"I have been meaning to write to you for a long time, to thank you for changing my life. Quick background: When I was 20 years old, I served a 2-year Mormon mission in the Philippines. Having seen all the custom sports uniforms made there, when I came home I started a business selling custom team apparel to high schools and colleges, in 2006, with $200.00 of capital, sleeping on the floor of my brother's living room. Also, with zero business experience and no one in my family with any, I went to BYU and majored in Entrepreneurship. I was named BYU's Entrepreneur of the Year, yet I graduated knowing nothing about marketing and selling. Graduated. Married. **Still with a struggling business. While looking for answers at Barnes & Noble, I came across your book** *No. B.S. Guide to Direct Marketing for Non-Direct Marketing Businesses.* **It blew my mind. Then I bought everything of yours I could afford. My business went from $50,000 a year to $2.5 million in just 5 years.** I am now in the process of selling my company to a big player in the industry for a multimillion-dollar sum, plus they want to bring me on as an executive at 4-times the salary I've been paying myself! You ARE 'The Millionaire Maker'!"

—Steve Rosenback, Garb Athletics

"It was Kennedy-style marketing that fueled an exceptional restaurant business. We received 64 People's Choice Awards, I gathered **over 63,000 customers,** I had 6 to 14 different promotions going on *simultaneously** each month (*a Renegade Millionaire lesson I learned from you), we grossed over $6.5 million a year with about $1 million in profits. An independent restaurant valuation firm analyzing the business for its sale said that, quote, less than 5 percent of the 945,000 food service establishments in the U.S. employ the advanced techniques and get the outstanding results Nakama has enjoyed as a direct result of its marketing. They stated that my restaurant was three times more successful than comparable restaurants because of my marketing. Ultimately, I sold the business. I'm beginning a new journey as an entrepreneur and a coach."

—Becky Auer, www.beckyauer.com

"My friend Dan Kennedy is unique, a genius in many ways. I have always admired his ability to see the vital truths in any business and to state these realities with straight language and clear definitions. His approach is direct. His ideas are controversial. **His ability to get results for his clients is unchallenged."**

—Brian Tracy, from his introduction to Dan's *No B.S. Business Success* book
Brian Tracy is one of America's most sought-after speakers and
the author of dozens of business books. www.BrianTracy.com

"Dan has literally eliminated the B.S. in explaining great ways to make more sales."

—Tom Hopkins, from his introduction to Dan's *No B.S. Sales Success* book
Tom Hopkins is world renowned as a master sales trainer. www.TomHopkins.com

THE N🚫B.S.
GUIDE TO
DIRECT MARKETING
FOURTH EDITION
BY
DAN S. KENNEDY

With Darcy Juarez and Marty Fort

& with special guest chapters from
Ben Glass and Craig Proctor

Entrepreneur
PRESS

Entrepreneur Press, Publisher
Cover Design: Andrew Welyczko
Production and Composition: Alan Barnett

This publication is designed to provide accurate and authoritative information in regard to the subject matter covered. It is sold with the understanding that the publisher is not engaged in rendering legal, accounting, or other professional services. If legal advice or other expert assistance is required, the services of a competent professional person should be sought.

Entrepreneur Press® is a registered trademark of Entrepreneur Media, LLC

Library of Congress Cataloging-in-Publication Data
Names: Kennedy, Dan S., author.
Title: No B.S. direct marketing for non-direct marketing businesses : the ultimate no holds barred kick butt take no prisoners guide to extraordinary growth & profits / by Dan Kennedy with Darcy Juarez and Marty Fort.
Description: Fourth edition. | [Irvine] : [Entrepreneur Press], [2024] | Includes index. | Summary: "In this updated and revised edition of No B.S. Direct Marketing, Dan builds on and re-affirms all the essential direct marketing strategies in the original edition, and adds new material addressing online, social and viral marketing media"-- Provided by publisher.
Identifiers: LCCN 2023043799 (print) | LCCN 2023043800 (ebook) | ISBN 9781642011685 (paperback) | ISBN 9781613084809 (epub)
Subjects: LCSH: Direct marketing. | Internet marketing. | Social media.
Classification: LCC HF5415.126 .K463 2024 (print) | LCC HF5415.126 (ebook) | DDC 658.8/72--dc23/eng/20231228
LC record available at https://lccn.loc.gov/2023043799
LC ebook record available at https://lccn.loc.gov/2023043800

CONTENTS

SECTION 1

FOUNDATION

CHAPTER 1
THE BIG SWITCH. Why Direct Marketing for NON-Direct Marketing Businesses?

SECTION 2

APPLICATION & EXAMPLES

Important Introduction by Dan Kennedy

The End of Advertising and Marketing as *You* Know It

I n the first edition of this book, back in 2006, before the recession, before the explosion of social media and the importance given to it as a marketing media, before all sorts of new media demanding business owners' attention, I wrote: Most small business advertising and marketing stinks. I said: Monstrous sums are wasted, and opportunities lost. My position hadn't changed by the time of the second edition or the third edition. As more and more and more ways to deliver advertising and marketing messages have been created and popularized, the effectiveness of it has declined, and the intelligence governing it has sunk to new lows. Now, as I write this, 17 years after the first edition, businesspeople are more the "advertising victims" than ever: confused and overwhelmed and hollered at, told that they *must* do this, that, the other thing, more and more—just to get the same results. Or less. I am here to mute the noise. To guide you to clarity, about a relatively short list of fundamental principles and strategies that can prevent your being lost in a deep, dense forest of media demanding your attention, time, and money.

In this edition, I invited my colleagues and friends Darcy Juarez and Marty Fort to take over some of the heavy lifting and update and freshen up many of the chapters. As you'll discover, they are both experienced, trustworthy guides to Direct Marketing. Marty transformed his local, retail brick-and-mortar businesses with it, and became a leader in his industry. Darcy has coached hundreds of business owners in applying Direct Marketing. Very hands-on. You'll learn more about them as they talk with you throughout this book.

Who to Model Your Marketing After

There is an old story about a motorist caught in the densest fog imaginable, unable to see anything but the taillights of the car in front of him, so he stayed very close, grateful for the guiding lights but fearful of falling back and having to navigate on his own. Suddenly the car in front came to a dead stop, and he rammed into the auto's rear. He jumped out, enraged, yelling at the driver he'd been following about the stupidity of making a sudden stop in such impenetrable fog. The guy said, "I'm sorry but I always come to a stop when pulling into my garage."

Modeling can be a powerful, efficient, and profitable strategy, *but only if you choose the right model.*

We can begin with the radical, challenging idea that just about everything you see BIG business doing is wrong for you—if you run a small business, a private practice, a service enterprise, or even a mid-sized, growth company. Big companies have different objectives, agendas, constituencies to satisfy, CEO egos to salve, as well as different resources and depth of resources than you do. If you study them at all, you must time travel to examine what they did in their journey from start to small and ultimately to big, not what they do now. If the rabbit emulates the lion, and sits on a rock, doesn't move, and roars loud and often, all the rabbit accomplishes is making it easier for predators to find him and eat him. A mouse using a lion as his model is a fool indeed.

It's also worth noting that, very often, the bigger a company grows, the dumber it gets. This is the result of having more and more people in it spending somebody's money other than their own and being safely distanced by bureaucracy from direct and immediate financial consequences from their decisions and from where the rubber meets road, on the store or showroom floor, face-to-face with customers, clients, or patients. These people are insulated from reality and very vulnerable to charlatanism prevalent inside ad agencies, social media agencies, and other shovel sellers. In the great Gold Rush, more money was made by the sellers of shovels—mules, mining equipment and tools, and maps—than by those actually searching for the gold. It's dressed up differently today, but the truth is unchanged.

At the time I wrote this, the news was filled with several big companies' costly blunders, one after another—notably Bud Light®, Target®, and Disney®. Billions of dollars of shareholder value was erased. If you were to have hastily followed their examples and had tried to apply their ideas to your advertising and marketing, you might have been bankrupt in a matter of months. Just because they are big does NOT mean their captains know what they are doing! I have sat in lavish, fancy offices at the top of skyscrapers with big, brand-name companies' CEOs and CMOs, and wondered how they could be so ignorant and foolish. As an investor, I worry a lot about stupidity at the top. About dumb following dumb.

Today, there are even a lot of retailers very visibly trying to build up their web presence and e-commerce, largely because Amazon has stepped into their territory in a big way, and because "everyone else is." They are often mystified and frustrated that they are losing money following Amazon, ignoring the fact that Amazon has and exploits truly unique advantages. The Amazon Factor is real, but blindly following Amazon as your model because they sell pet supplies and you have stores that do, too, is a fast track to disaster. Many seeming e-commerce merchants aren't being fed by online media either. You may see a company like Boll & Branch (luxury bedding) or a charity like Tunnel to Towers as e-commerce and pointed to by sellers of online advertising as proof of its power, but much of their online traffic is being created offline, with direct-response radio, TV, print, and direct mail. Hard-core, classic, principled direct-response, adhering to and demonstrating the approach I'm giving you in this book. Be cautious about crediting too much significance to any big company's observed activities or methods, to any business seeming to be driven by online advertising, to Amazon, and most important of all, to your own peers who are influenced by inappropriate models.

The fact is that most of your peers are blind mice leading other blind mice. The proof is in the financial facts of every category of business, every profession, every sales organization, every population: 1 percent create tremendous incomes and wealth; 4 percent do very well; 15 percent earn good livings; 60 percent stall, stagnate, and struggle endlessly; and 20 percent fail. Working back up, you have an 80 percent poor vs. 20 percent prosperous ratio, a 95 percent vs. 5 percent, or even a 99 percent vs. 1 percent ratio. Thus, the overwhelming majority of your peers are engaged in marketing that fails them, intellectually and emotionally committed to that failed and failing marketing, and bloated with opinions about why you should follow the same path to frustration and failure. If you refuse, deviate, or even dare to question the validity of this path, your peers and friends and sometimes employees react violently. They mock, they criticize, they shame, they shun. It's important to remember that every critic has his own agenda, whether conscious or subconscious.

Here are the facts that prove the majority is wrong about anything having to do with money:

Figure P. 1: The Money Pyramid

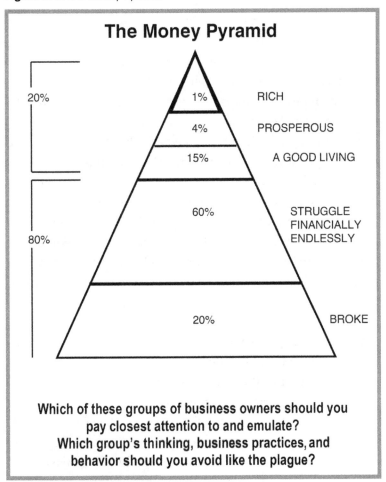

Crossing the Great Divide
of Advertising and Marketing

The principle that what you see others doing is not necessarily what you should be doing—especially if they have a different agenda than yours—is a challenging idea.

Next, I offer the even more radical and challenging idea that pretty much everything you think you know and have been conditioned to believe about marketing is wrong. Here, I am going to expose the Great Divide.

On one side, the majority of companies and business owners who are married to very traditional, mainstream, brand– and name visibility–driven, largely unaccountable advertising and marketing. Most of the money invested in it is based on faith and hope. Many people think, falsely, that by using new media they are doing a new kind of marketing. In truth, they merely move the same bad advertising and flawed marketing from one place to another. Also on this side are a lot of big, dumb companies with mixed and mixed-up agendas, with marketing media and message decisions driven by top executives' ego, by the need to impress Wall Street bankers, by pursuit of favorable recognition in their industry. Sometimes there are legitimate in-industry political considerations. All this puts accountable return on investment low on their priorities, but for you, it probably is or should be Priority #1.

On the other side, a smaller ragtag band of rebels and rogues and renegades who utilize *Direct* Marketing. This book will expose the Great Divide between the two. Moons ago, the greatest ad man of the Mad Men era, David Ogilvy, credited us—the direct marketing rogues—with being the only people using advertising who actually knew what we were doing. He made this pronouncement despite leading a traditional ad agency, as a criticism of his own people and of his own clients!

He was right then. It's truer now. Most, yes, *most* of what you see done in advertising and marketing is being done by people who *don't know* what they are doing.

If you get it, really get this, you'll smack yourself in the head for not seeing it all sooner, on your own. You'll be in awe of how much sense it makes. You'll never look at an ad, sales letter, website, etc. the same way again. You'll be ruined toward traditional advertising for life. You will make major changes in your own advertising and marketing—fast. When you do, you *will* be argued with, ridiculed, and criticized by employees, peers, competitors, maybe even family and friends. You will need depth of understanding about Direct Marketing to stay strong. The astounding results you'll see from full conversion from Ordinary Marketing to Direct Marketing will convince you, but know you will need courage and discipline to stay your new course. I promise you that being thought of as a fool or a misguided renegade and having millions of dollars trumps being thought of as "normal" and "correct" and "proper" and barely making a living!

For the record, my private clients combined invest at least $500 million a year in advertising and marketing following my advice and methodology or having me at the helm, but most are small businesses, groups of small businesses, private practices, groups of private practices—not huge entities. Entrepreneurs getting their companies onto the Inc. 5000 list, not the Fortune 500 list. Significantly, 85 percent of all clients who work with me once do so continuously or episodically, that fact spanning over 50 years. I get nearly obscene amounts of money to advise entrepreneurs exclusively on Direct Marketing, and to craft sales copy and marketing systems for them. My current fees begin at $19,400 for consulting days, for repeat clients, and $21,000 for first-time clients. Project fees range upwards from $100,000 to $1 million plus royalties.

I am semi-retired, having experienced some medical crises that forced me to make changes in the way I work and the quantity of it that I do. I am busier than I wish to be. I tell you this not to brag, but to impress on you the extremely high value of the information in this book. I know how to produce RESULTS. Not brand awareness, visibility, likes, followers, or other fools' metrics. Results. *Money.* Nothing, and I mean NOTHING can have as positive and as dramatic an impact on your prosperity as crossing the Great Divide to being a Direct Marketer—regardless of your particular products or services, other deliverables, or size of your business. This book is not about doing *better* marketing. It is about a total conversion to entirely *different* marketing.

Down from the Top of the Success Mountain, the Ten Commandments of Direct Marketing (For *Non*-Direct Marketing Businesses)

You will get "THE RULES" from me. (The "Ten Commandments" are on Page 25.) All my life I've been a rule-breaker, so laying down these Rules is a bit odd. But when all this is new, it's best to have strict and rigid and relatively simple Rules to adhere to. With depth of understanding, successful experience, and ability, you can later inject creativity and innovation and develop a system uniquely your own. For now, my Rules will rule.

I am often asked about flexibility, and often criticized for my rigidity about these Rules. Let me be absolutely clear: Anybody who argues for flexibility and encourages you to inject your own *opinions* into this is a danger to themselves and others. The next time you fly across the country, pray your pilot is rigidly, unerringly adhering to The Rules for takeoff, flight, and landing. Pray he doesn't think it'd be more interesting to fly upside down, sideways, blindfolded, or after having a couple whiskey and sodas. His strict, perfect adherence to THE Rules is vital. Yes, Captain Sully famously threw out the rule book and defied protocol for his miracle landing on the Hudson River. Let's see that done ten times in a row. Also, he was under extreme duress in a dire crisis. You should want to do things that work consistently, ten times, ten thousand times in a row, and with which success and profit is *not a miracle*! For that, you will master and adhere to The Rules that I share here. You will master an entire, a-to-z process based on these Rules. And you will see Examples here in this book, and suggested for you to go and see online, that demonstrate and prove The Rules. Out the back of all this, **you will be able to transform your business to an infinitely more powerful Direct Marketing business—*if you dare.***

Meet the Authors

DAN S. KENNEDY is a multimillionaire serial entrepreneur, sought-after Direct Marketing consultant and Direct-Response Advertising copywriter, author of numerous business books including the No B.S. series, and founder of the No B.S. / Magnetic Marketing membership organization and its flagship newsletter, the *No B.S. Marketing Letter*. His long speaking career included 9 years on tour, 20+ cities a year, audiences of 15,000 to 25,000 with 4 former U.S. presidents, Hollywood and sports celebrities, legendary entrepreneurs and CEOs, and top business speakers Zig Ziglar, Brian Tracy, and Tom Hopkins. His own events have featured celebrity entrepreneurs like Gene Simmons (KISS), Kathy Ireland, George Foreman, and Joan Rivers. He is semi-retired, with a small Private Client Group he advises via tele-consulting; he also continuously contributes to Magnetic Marketing, makes speaking appearances for Magnetic Marketing and Click Funnels, and occasionally accepts an interesting new client. He can be reached via fax at 330-908-0250 or at 154 E. Aurora Rd. #353, Northfield, Ohio 44067. (Mr. Kennedy does not use email.)

DARCY JUAREZ is a strategist and implementer of all things Direct Marketing. Working with solo entrepreneurs and small businesses, she has built marketing funnels, written sales copy, written and ghostwritten books, created info-kits and shock-and-awe packages, built websites, and created and managed major online product launches. In addition to her freelance work with private clients, she is the Chief Business Strategist at Magnetic Marketing and actively involved with members of its coaching groups. Darcy contributes monthly to the *No B.S. Marketing Letter*. She can be found at www.DarcyJuarez.com.

MARTY FORT owns and operates the largest community music schools in South Carolina, serving over 1,600 students and involving 80 music teachers. His schools' students have performed at Carnegie Hall, Graceland, and the Rock & Roll Hall of Fame. Marty shares the unusual and unusually successful Direct-Response Advertising and Direct Marketing he uses for his schools with thousands of school owners through his Music Academy Success® coaching program, seminars, and publications. He is the inventor of the Music Ladder Success System® used by more than 30,000 music students nationwide, recipient of nine patents, and author of the #1 Amazon best-selling book *The Ultimate Guide to Music Lessons*. He also holds leadership positions at Magnetic Marketing, with mastermind and coaching groups of owners of very diverse businesses, and contributes monthly to the *No B.S. Marketing Letter*. He can be found at MusicAcademySuccess.com.

SECTION 1

FOUNDATION

The Big Switch

Why Direct Marketing for NON-Direct Marketing Businesses?

by Dan Kennedy

I t is an odd sort of title, isn't it?

If you picked it up hoping for huge breakthroughs in your business, you bought the right book. But first, I have to get these definitions out of the way.

By *non*-direct marketing business, I mean anything but a mail-order, catalog, or online marketer who *directly* solicits orders for merchandise. It could be a local dental practice, carpet cleaning business, brick-and-mortar retailer, B2B—IT consultant, CPA firm, industrial equipment manufacturer. The owners of such businesses do not think of themselves as direct marketers engaged in Direct-Response Advertising, until I get ahold of them!

Examples of pure Direct Marketing businesses just about everybody knows are the TV home shopping channels QVC and HSN, catalogers like J. Peterman or Hammacher Schlemmer, and contemporary catalog and online catalog/e-commerce companies like Amazon; businesses like Fruit of the Month Club; and mass users of direct-mail to sell things like Publishers Clearinghouse. In recent years, MyPillow® and Balance of Nature® have exploded onto the Direct Marketing scene. As I write this, you can't watch an hour of cable TV news without being besieged by their ads. Organizations like AARP and charities like Wounded Warrior, Tunnel to Towers, St. Jude's, and even local food banks are Direct Marketers.

Online media like YouTube and TikTok have challenged traditional gatekeeper and distribution channels, and a number of musicians, comedians, other entertainers, authors, and others have "gone direct," becoming Direct Marketers without necessarily thinking of themselves as such.

There are tens of thousands of true Direct Marketing businesses. Some are familiar to the general public; many, many more are familiar only to the niche or special interest they serve. For example, at any given moment, I have over 50 direct marketers as clients, each selling books, audio CDs, and downloads; home study courses and seminars and services by mail; internet and print media; and teleseminars and webinars, which market only to a specific industry or profession—one to carpet cleaners, another to restaurant owners, another to chiropractors, etc. If you are not in one of these niches, you probably have no idea there is as much Direct Marketing going on as there is. If you don't own a music school, you're unlikely to know about Marty Fort's Music Success Academy®. If you're not a dentist, you're unlikely to know about my client Dr. David Phelps and Freedom Founders. There are also Direct Marketers unknown by name but known by their products or brands, like a longtime client of mine, Guthy-Renker Corporation, the billion-dollar Pro-Activ® acne creams, skincare product Crepe Erase, and many other products made into brands by Direct Marketing. What all these have in common is their fundamental process of selling direct via media to consumers, with no brick-and-mortar locations or face-to-face contact required. There are brands that start with pure Direct Marketing that later expand to their own stores or other retail distribution, like Warby Parker and Untuckit®.

Direct Marketing is everywhere, making fortunes for national marketers in every category but strangely, oddly, weirdly copied by very, very few local businesses in those same categories. Omaha Steaks® is the leading national, mail-order butcher shop, but hardly any local butcher shops or supermarket meat departments copy its successful advertising and marketing methods. Why? I do not know. But I do know that this strange situation is YOUR great opportunity.

This book is for the owner of a brick-and-mortar business, a business with a store, showroom, or office, a restaurant, a dental practice, an accounting practice, or a funeral home—that is, some kind of ordinary business, one most likely local and serving a local market. These are the entrepreneurs who have populated my audiences for five decades, subscribe to my newsletters, and use my systems to **transform those "ordinary" businesses into extraordinary money machines that far, far out-perform their industry norms, peers, competitors, and their own wildest imaginations. How do they do it? The big switch is a simple one to state (if more complex to do): They switch from traditional advertising to** *Direct-Response* **Advertising. They stop emulating ordinary and traditional marketing and instead emulate** *Direct* **Marketing.**

Most "ordinary" businesses advertise and market like much bigger brand-name companies, so they spend (waste) a lot of money on image, brand, and presence. But copycatting these big brand-name companies is a rabbit behaving like the lion. It makes *no* sense. The big companies have all sorts of reasons for the way they advertise and market that have nothing to do with getting a customer or making sales! Because your agenda is much simpler, you should find successful businesses with similar agendas to copycat. Those are direct marketers. You and they share the same basic ideas:

1. Spend $1 on marketing, get back $2 or $20, fast, that can be accurately tracked to the $1 spent.
2. Do NOT spend $1 that does not directly and quickly bring back $2 or $20.

Big Company's Agenda for Advertising and Marketing

1. Please/appease its board of directors (most of whom know zip about advertising and marketing but have lots of opinions).

2. Please/appease its stockholders.

3. Look good, look appropriate to Wall Street.

4. Look good, appropriate to the media.

5. Build brand identity.

6. Win awards for advertising.

7. Sell something.

Your Agenda

1. Sell something. Now.

Please stop and be sure you get this life-changing principle. Be careful who you copy. Be careful who you act like. Be careful who you study. If their purpose, objectives, agenda, reasons for doing what they do the way they do it don't match up with your purpose, objectives, agenda, then you should NOT study or emulate or copy them!

Please stop and be sure you get this life-changing corollary principle. Find somebody who is successful, who shares your purpose, objectives, agenda, and pay great attention to what he does and how he does it.

I believe some call this sort of thing "a blinding flash of the obvious." Well, you can call it obvious if you like—but then how do you explain the fact that 99 percent of all businesspeople are operating as if they are ignorant of this obvious logic?

I might add, this principle has power in places other than marketing. You *can* eventually get south by going due north, but life's easier and less stressful, and business more profitable, if you actually get headed in the direction that leads directly to your destination of choice. Emulating inappropriate examples is the equivalent of trudging south to get to the North Pole. Odds are, you'll get lost, tired, or eaten by a giant iguana long before seeing snow.

Why Is There So Much Lousy, Unproductive, Unprofitable Advertising and Marketing Out There, Anyway?

No B.S. truth. Most business owners are just about clueless when it comes to advertising and marketing. They are therefore often *Advertising Victims*, preyed on by media salespeople, ad agencies, website developers, social media wizards, and others who don't know any more about how to actually produce a customer or make a sale than they do. Anytime you are being guided to decisions and investments that are not *fact* based, but instead driven by popular fads, trends, opinions, monkey-see-monkey-do pressure, you are being victimized. Direct Marketers insist on facts and live by data.

If you try to get a business owner to accurately tell you where his customers and sales come from, what it costs to get a customer from source A or source B, what results specifically come from this ad or that one, he can't. He's guessing. Consequently, he's often grumpy and unhappy about things he shouldn't be, but also wasting money he needn't be.

The reasons for the cluelessness and vulnerability to victimization are many. Here's a big one: *Marketing Incest.* When you got into whatever business you're in, you probably looked around at what everybody else in the business was doing and copied it. Gradually, you've tried to do it better, but not radically different, just better. So you have everybody in an industry standing in a circle looking inward at each other, ignoring anyone or anything outside the circle. It's incestuous, and it works just like real generational incest: Everybody slowly gets dumber and dumber and dumber.

This book dares you to turn your back on the circle and deliberately go far afield from your peers in search of different—not just incrementally better—*different* ways of marketing.

Yes, Salvation Is within Reach

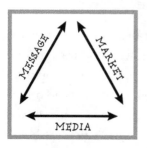

Now, here's the good news: Most business owners, clueless as they may be about profitable advertising or effective marketing, do know a lot about how to *sell* their products or services. That's very good news because *DIRECT Marketing for NON-Direct*

Marketing Businesses is really not about traditional advertising or marketing at all. It is simply "salesmanship multiplied in media." So you actually already do have a firm grip on one-third of the KENNEDY RESULTS TRIANGLE that you'll master with this book. You know the Message. It'll get tweaked, as I'll explain. But you do have this component part.

The 10 No B.S. Rules of Direct Marketing for Non-Direct Marketing Businesses (My Ten Commandments)

I'll lay our foundation first. (A radical idea itself!) Please copy these and post them somewhere you'll see them often until you get them memorized. Doing so will keep you on track, save you a lot of money, and dramatically improve your marketing.

From now on, every ad you run, every flyer you distribute, every postcard or letter you mail, every website you put up, every/anything you do to advertise or market your business MUST adhere to these rules. To be fair, they are simplistic and dogmatic, and there are reasons to violate them in certain situations. But for now, sticking to them as a rigid diet will work. You can experiment later, after you've first cleansed your business of toxins.

Rule #1:	There Will Aways Be an Offer or Offer(s)
Rule #2:	There Will Be a Reason to Respond Right Now
Rule #3:	You Will Give Clear Instructions
Rule #4:	There Will Be Tracking, Measurement, and Accountability
Rule #5:	Only No-Cost Brand-Building

Rule #6:	There Will Be Follow-Up
Rule #7:	There Will Be Strong Copy
Rule #8:	It Will Look Like Mail-Order Advertising
Rule #9:	Results Rule. Period.
Rule #10:	You Will Be a Tough-Minded Disciplinarian and Put Your Business on a Strict Direct Marketing Diet

We'll tackle each Rule in depth, in the next 10 chapters.

I wrote an entire book about breaking rules, *NO B.S. GUIDE TO SUCCEEDING IN BUSINESS BY BREAKING ALL THE RULES*, and generally speaking, I think rules are for other, ordinary mortals—certainly not for me, and not for you either if you are a true entrepreneur. So you'll chafe at rules here just as I would. However, when you are attempting to undo bad habits and replace them with new ones, some hard and fast rules are necessary, temporarily. Once you fully understand these and have lived with them for a reasonable length of time, then feel free to experiment if you wish. But get good at coloring inside the lines before ignoring them altogether.

Finally, a word about these aged rules and the newest of the new media and its promoters of new metrics. Try putting views or likes on a bank deposit slip. You will be told that *no* old rules—the time-tested, time-proven ones—apply to new media like Facebook or Twitter/X or websites, etc., but be certain to take into account who makes that argument. It will come from young people on your staff or in agencies spending your money, not theirs, unable if pressed to prove profitable return on investment from their chosen media and made-up metrics. When pressed on this point, they won't argue facts because they can't; they will only stigmatize and label you as a dummy and a primitive stuck in the past's old ways. It will come from people caught up in a dumb cattle stampede: *You have to do it and throw harsh reality accountability aside because everybody else is doing it* and ignoring financial accountability. It will come from peddlers of it for profit. Of course, the bald man should never ask the hungry barber if he needs a haircut. When all you have to sell are haircuts, everyone needs them.

Now, we'll tackle each Rule in order...

CHAPTER 2

An OFFER They Can't Refuse

By Marty Fort

There is a certain mindset in Direct Marketing folks. We are result oriented. We want to KNOW if we have won or lost, succeeded or failed, achieved something definitive or just wandered around. While this tendency gets in the way of a friendly family game night, it is extremely useful in avoiding the vagueness and lack of accountability that permeates most business owners' marketing activities. Traditional and brand or image advertising defies accountability. It is difficult to know what it is producing. With Direct-Response Advertising, we can know. Here's how:

Rule 1:
There Will ALWAYS Be an Offer or Offers

A key distinguishing characteristic of Direct Marketing and Direct-Response Advertising from all other marketing and advertising is the presentation of a very specific offer or offers. Ideally, yours is a Godfather's Offer—an offer that the appropriate prospect or customer for you *can't* refuse! We'll get to the architecture of offers in a few minutes, but first the overarching ideas: One, to make your *every* communication actually ask somebody to do something specific, and two, to inject new disciplines of selling and accountability into *all* your communication with prospects, customers, and the marketplace at large.

I have built two very successful businesses—my three music schools and my business coaching hundreds of other school owners—by absolute adherence to this Rule. Later in the Applications Section, I show you and talk you through one of my evergreen offers, which I use consistently, and have for years. I make sure that I know the exact results from each ad, mailing, online promotion, every media so that I can reuse and increase frequency of use or expand range of media used with a winner, and so I can bury the losers with no hesitation.

If you begin paying attention to advertising and marketing, you'll see that most of it merely shows up and talks about the marketers and advertisers, but does not directly offer something specific to be had by immediately and directly responding. A lot of print ads and TV commercials and brochures include social media sites, websites, Facebook sites where you can go follow them, like them, etc., but present no offer as a compelling reason to go there. All this is *undisciplined*. It is sending money out to play a backyard game with no score-keeping, no clear means of judging victory or defeat. When you take this undisciplined approach and simply spend and hope and guess, you're at the mercy of opinion about your marketing: Do you like it? Does your mother-in-law like it? Do your customers say nice things about it? Try paying any of your bills with that sort of feedback.

The only way you can know what works is with specific offers for which the response can be accurately tracked. Whether it's my music schools or a church or a professional practice, offers are essential. They are essential not just because they create results, but also because they impose discipline.

Direct Marketing imposes discipline. That discipline may be as important and valuable as the benefit of direct response itself. For some mysterious reason, business owners are willing to let advertising and marketing off the hook, but tend to hold everything else accountable for results and return on investment. If they tie up money in certain product inventory, they expect it to sell—or they refuse to restock it. If they employ a sales representative, they expect him to make sales. If they buy a delivery van, they expect it to start and run so it can make deliveries. If they pay a laborer by the hour, they expect him to clock in, be there, and work for the hour. Yet, investments made for marketing are permitted to skate. Only Direct Marketing imposes discipline, by always making an offer or offers, so the response to those offers can be tracked and measured, injecting factual accountability.

I'll tell you a true story about accountability and the anti-accountability forces that are out there against us. I was at a radio station taping a commercial. I said at the end of the script, "If you want to claim this special offer, say that you heard about it on this radio station." When I did that, I was literally surrounded immediately by four brass, top dogs at the radio station who stormed into the studio. They said, "You can't say, 'Did you hear about it on this station?'" I said I either leave this ad as is or I walk. We either put in the tagline or cancel the entire campaign. Here's the dirty little secret : The reason they did not want me to use the tracking language is *they don't want their advertisers to know whether their advertising is working or not.* They rely on an "anti-accountability" mindset. Whether it's radio, TV, print, social media, any marketing source I always track. You will get pushback from print media. You will get pushback from radio and TV ad execs. You will get censorship and pushback from social media with various algorithms. But if you're going to make it all the way with Direct Marketing, tracking must be fought for and must be utilized at all levels and with all marketing campaigns.

Let's be clear about this: You are investing real money. Why wouldn't you demand a real result?

You'll notice now that the radio and TV industry has been brought to cooperating with this. Most direct-response ads tell you to use a particular promo code or use the show host's name when responding. Tracking has imposed its will thanks to big Direct Marketers. But should you hire an ad or social media agency, you'll find, 99 out of 100 times, resistance to direct offers and tracking. You will find an anti-accountability bias. They don't want to know, and they don't want you to know.

One of the all-time speaking greats, Zig Ziglar, always described salespeople who wimped out at closing sales and directly demanding orders as "professional *visitors,*" not professional salespeople. Since you will be doing selling in print, online, with media, you rarely want to let it be a professional visitor on your behalf. Fire all the wimps. Demand real performance. Incorporate a specific offer each and every time you put out a message, of any kind, by any means.

I mean of *any* kind, by *any* means. At Magnetic Marketing, we teach most business owners to use Thanksgiving greeting cards and/or New Year's greeting cards, with past and lost as well as active customers, clients, or patients, and, often, with unconverted leads, too. We also teach that no greeting card should arrive without being accompanied by an offer. Typically, the offer will be a gift with a visit to the showroom or store, a gift with the purchase, a gift for referral, etc., placed in a printed piece inside a separate envelope, inside the greeting card itself, to preserve some separation between the thank-you or new-year sentiment and selling. But: **We are *not* shy about our purpose in life either, and it is not merely being professional visitors.**

In short, you have a fundamental governance decision to make. Will you let yourself be persuaded or bullied into wasting money on marketing that cannot be *directly* held accountable for results and return on investment? Or will you insist on accountability?

Figure 2.1: Example of Direct Mail Card with Gift Inside:

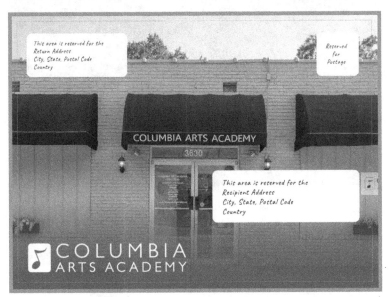

Dear [[Firstname]],

HAPPY BIRTHDAY from all of us at the Columbia Arts Academy!

Come back and make music with us by signing up or lessons and we'll give you your first lesson for free and a free registration. $57.50 in savings. You can also give this to a friend or family member.

Wishing you an AMAZING birthday and let's MAKE MUSIC!

MARTY FORT
Founder and President
Columbia Arts Academy

803-667-4451
3630 Rosewood Dr, Columbia, SC
info@columbiaartsacademy.com
columbiaartsacademy.com

AREA RESERVED FOR RETURN ADDRESS
AND BARCODE

How to Do It: Two Types of Offers

There are basically two types of offers. There is an offer requesting purchase. There is also the lead generation offer, asking only for a person to, in effect, raise their hand, to identify and register themselves as having interest in a certain subject matter and information or goods or services, and to invite further communication from you. Often, although not always, the lead generation offer is free. There are times and places for both kinds of offers, but no communication should be without some offer.

The Direct Purchase Offer

A lot of marketing, online and offline, uses some of the simplest, most straightforward direct purchase offers, like "Buy One, Get One Free"—used by everybody from pizza shops to window replacement companies. Discounting as a strategy can be very dangerous. Another common direct purchase offer, in place of or combined with discounting, is gift with purchase. These were birthed by direct marketers but have migrated to retail, service, professions, and B2B, so they are commonplace. They should be and usually are married to a hard deadline. They provide an easy opportunity to accurately measure their effectiveness and production, although out of ignorance or laziness, many business owners fail to measure.

Direct Purchase Offers have several significant disadvantages. One is that they tend to sacrifice price integrity and profitability, and if relied on too frequently, train customers to only respond when a "great deal" is offered. Two, they can only be responded to by people ready and able to buy right this minute—they fail to identify people likely to buy in your category in the near future. Third, they can be easily and quickly comparison shopped, especially if you are conveying the offer online. Still, business does revolve around Direct Purchase Offers.

Figure 2.2: Example of a Direct Purchase Offer:

The Lead Generation Offer

This is a more interesting kind of offer, because it can substantially reduce the waste factor in advertising, convert a sales culture to a marketing culture, and provide opportunity to build trust and develop customers.

You see lead generation done by Direct Marketers routinely and regularly. You may not have given them much thought, but now you will. They are commonly used by national direct marketers but rarely used by local, small businesses—even though the national and local firms may be in the same product or service categories. For example, a company like Premier Bathtubs, which sells walk-in bathtubs that are safer for elderly people, advertises just about everywhere, offering a free information kit with brochures and a DVD. Once somebody raises their hand and registers themselves as interested in making a home's bathroom safe for themselves or an elderly parent, the company has a marketing opportunity. Oddly, you will almost never catch a local remodeling company duplicating this strategy. Instead, they tend to leap to offering an in-home estimate for work to be done. This is often A Bridge Too Far.

I'm a big believer in the concept of *development*. Accumulating leads, nurturing them, working them, dripping information on them, and maximizing the marketing opportunity. In my brick-and-mortar businesses, we see people come in months, even years after they have first requested information for music lessons. The one thing entrepreneurs do not have is any kind of patience. We all want sales and we want them right now. If you do want to speed that process up, follow-up systems via your staff, media, and technology are key.

You can have both: immediate sales with buy-now customers PLUS building a bank of not-yet-ready customers you develop over time. With the right lead generation offers, you can attract both the eager-to-buy-now customer and quickly bring him to a point of sale AND you can attract a lot of curious, interested, persuadable not-yet-ready future buyers.

This gets you more value for your advertising or marketing dollars. In his Renegade Millionaire System®, Dan teaches this as an application of his Present Bank / Future Bank / Simultaneous Deposit Strategy.

The Important Concept of Threshold Resistance & How to Increase Response to Offers

Arnold Taubman, one of America's most successful mall developers, spoke and wrote at length about the concept of Threshold Resistance as it applies to entrances to retail stores and window displays of retail stores. I find it applies even more broadly to Direct Marketing. All offers fall somewhere on a continuum between Low Threshold Offer and High Threshold Offer.

Figure 2.3: Threshold Resistance

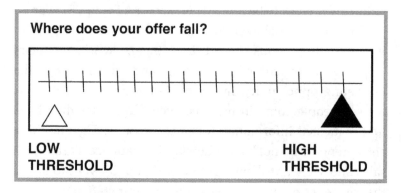

Here are examples of Offers that would fall somewhere between Middle and High on the spectrum:

Chiropractor   Free Exam

Financial Advisor   Free Seminar

Remodeler   Free Estimate

Restaurant   Promotional Offer (e.g., BOGO or Free Appetizer with…)

These score toward High Threshold because they can be scary and intimidating to the consumer. They require people to put themselves in uncomfortable positions. They require a decision nearly made—to get care, to find an advisor, to get remodeling done, or try a restaurant they've never patronized before, where they can't be sure of a good experience. A great many people with evolving interest or interest that can be stimulated will still not be prepared to take this big of a step forward. You have no way of knowing how many people noticed your advertising and gave it some thought, but stopped short of acting on it because of its high threshold resistance. I can promise you—it's a lot!

Examples of Low Threshold Offers

Nothing happens until somebody responds! You don't know they are good potential customers so you can't do anything constructive to move them toward you. This is why so many Direct Marketers use low resistance offers. They just want a response, *then* the game can begin.

The lowest threshold offer is for free information, to be sent by mail or Federal Express, or accessed online. This is *the* staple item of Direct-Response Advertising, in virtually every category of business. The largest wealth management firm, Fisher Investments, on TV and radio, in *Forbes* and other magazines; one of the most successful home improvement product manufacturers, SunSetter Awnings, by direct-mail and blow-in inserts in magazines and newspapers; one of the biggest health insurers, Humana, in TV commercials; virtually all of the companies like my Music Academy Success® information and coaching business and even academic institutions such as High Point University all offer low threshold, information items like books, free reports, DVDs, complete information kits, e-books, e-reports, webinars. If this is their #1 strategy, why shouldn't it be yours? Keep in mind, these are big, national direct-response advertisers who have plenty of opportunity to run split-tests often, and do, and keep returning to the tried-and-true, low threshold, free information offer.

Use "Information First Marketing," Not Product or Service First

Dan Kennedy first coined the term "Information <u>First</u> Marketing" for this. Really savvy local business operators are embracing it, modeling the national advertisers. This is a wave of change not just in the way businesses advertise to attract new customers, but in *what* they advertise. The karate school *doesn't* advertise itself, its lessons, or a free lesson. Instead, it advertises a free report by its owner: *The Parents' Guide to Cyber-Bullying and Bullying: Raising Emotionally Strong Kids.* The mattress store *doesn't* advertise itself, its mattresses, or some sale of the century. It advertises its free guidebook: *Why You Can't Seem to Get a Good Night's Sleep.* The IT consultant *doesn't* advertise his services. He advertises a free book: *You Are the Target: Cybersecurity before It's Too Late.*

And the same is true with my coaching program, Music Academy Success®. If you look at our entry point, we offer a free report: *The 16 Keys That Will Unlock the Hidden Profits in Your Music School.* It's a tried-and-true low threshold offer, and here's an example.

One of my very good friends, Grandmaster Stephen Oliver, is a 9th degree black belt. He is a coach to the martial arts industry and is now also coaching financial advisors. If you want some insight on how to create low threshold offers, he's a good guy to study. On one of our Magnetic Marketing Challenges, he talked about just this phenomenon. He said that being a high degree black belt or what type of martial arts is taught is irrelevant to prospective students or parents.

They don't know what that means. What matters more is what the parents want for their kids—like confidence, self-esteem, safety. Examples include, "Is my son going to be bullied? Is my daughter going to suffer depression? Is my teen thinking about self-harm?" And on and on. If you stop thinking about the world through your lens and start thinking about it through your customers' lens, you can imagine a number of subjects and titles for Info-First Marketing for your type of business. If you stop thinking about the product or service you want to sell and, instead, think about the questions, concerns, problems, and desires you can *first* raise with your potential customers you will gain enormous competitive advantages.

The Hybrid Approach

There is no law that says you must choose just one of these approaches.

Most advertising dramatically suppresses possible response by presenting only a single reason for said response. Typically, this is a High Threshold Offer that requires somebody to be 99.9 percent ready to buy now. Nobody's coming in for a $59 exam, or a free exam, unless they are 99 percent ready to put a chiropractic physician to work on their back pain today. But a lot of people suffering with nagging or episodically reoccurring back pain, who are having evolving thoughts about doing something about it, would respond to a Low Threshold Offer of information about *Best Ways to Relieve Nagging Back Pain—Without Surgery or Drugs.* You don't have to be dead or have a dead family member in the dining room to respond to a Low Threshold Offer from a funeral parlor. One ad can present the usual stuff—here we are, here's what we do; if you have an immediate need, call this number anytime 24 hours a day, 7 days a week and one of our professionals will be immediately available to assist you—*but also present* the Low Threshold Offer, too, as shown here:

For a free "Pre-Need Planning Kit" and Special Report:
19 Financial and Estate Planning Tips for Responsible Family Leaders,
Visit www.planwisely.com or call 000-000-0000.
It will be sent by mail, no cost, no obligation.

To be clear, here's what I've introduced you to here:
1. The use of offers
2. The difference between Low to High Threshold Offers
3. The use of Lead Generation Offers
4. Single Reason to Respond vs. Multiple Reasons to Respond

Once a business owner understands these things, his objection is often about possible trade-down of response. The fear is that somebody who might call or come in or otherwise respond to a High Threshold Offer and make an immediate purchase will trade down to a Low Threshold Offer and delay his purchase or be scooped up by a competitor. While this does happen, it usually affects far fewer people than a business owner fears, and the improved total response and value of leads captured for development more than makes up for what little trade-down occurs. After all, the person who fell off a ladder and has to crawl to the phone isn't going to trade down from making an appointment with the doctor to requesting a free report or registering for a webinar next Tuesday. The person with a dead body on hand is unlikely to trade down from immediate assistance at the funeral parlor to getting a free Info-Kit. In most cases, you can safely add Low Threshold Offers without significantly compromising response to a High Threshold Offer designed for the person ready to buy now.

Ultimately, your decisions about the nature of your offer(s), where they fall on the Low to High Threshold continuum, whether or not they feature information, whether they are for lead generation or immediate purchase activity or a hybrid of the two are situational. Different media, different markets, different timing will color those decisions. You should realize you have choices and you can make your marketing dollars work harder for you by offering people more than one reason and more than one means of responding to you. But, no matter what you make of these choices each time you must make them in putting forward marketing, your pledge of honor to Rule #1 must be: There will *always* be an offer or offers.

Rule 2:
There Will Be Reason to Respond Right Now

Hesitation and procrastination are among the most common of all human behaviors.

If you are a mail-order catalog shopper, you have—more than once—browsed, folded down corners of pages from which you intended to buy items, set the catalogs aside, and never placed the orders. This happens with every marketing media. People watching a TV infomercial almost buy, but put it off, to do the next time they see it, or jot down the 800-number, to do it later, but later never comes. A shopper enters the mall, sees an outfit she likes, but tells herself she'll stop and look at it and probably get it on her way out. By the time she has walked the mall, had lunch, bought other items, and is headed back to the end of the mall where she entered, she is focused on getting to her car and getting home. The dress spotted on arrival is left behind. This "effect" is even worse with consumers shopping around online. They can easily get lost in search, in social media, on YouTube, etc., and experience the paradox of choice; too many so the escape is putting any response off until "later."

We must be sharply, painfully aware of all the potential response lost to such hesitation. The hidden cost and failure in all advertising and marketing is with *the Almost-Persuaded.* They were tempted to respond. They nearly responded. They got right up to the edge of response, but then set it aside to take care of later or to mull over or to Google when they have time. When they get to that edge, we must reach across and pull them past it. There must be good reason for them not to stop short or delay or ponder. There must be *urgency.*

Direct Marketing can often *contextually* **provide urgency of immediate response.** This can be done with limited supply, limit per household or buyer, or the countdown clock you see on a direct-response TV commercial or a webinar. If the product itself cannot be limited in supply, some bonus or premium attached to it certainly can be. In the seminar and event business, a place I live and work, we use the obvious devices like "early bird discounts" and extend-a-pay monthly installments tied to a deadline to motivate early registrations, but we also use bonuses, entries into prize drawings, backstage pass opportunities, preferred seating, and closed-door, limited-number luncheon tickets available only to the first 50 or first 100 to beat the deadline. Retail mimics this with the "door buster sales" starting at 5 a.m., 6 a.m., or 7 a.m., and can add to that urgency with a gift for the first x-number to be there with noses pressed against the glass. Amazon does it with its yearly Prime Day(s) featuring new, special offers every hour. All these examples are about creating *a context for urgency of response.*

With Info-First, lead generation, advertising some impending crisis or imminent danger or some new opportunity that must be acted on quickly, is often used. The idea of getting in on the ground floor and being ahead of all others is a tried-and-true appeal, now commonly called FOMO. A coming doom often works even better. Either way, you offer information they must have now, before they do anything or make any decisions in your category—for example: "**Before you file your income taxes this year**, you need these seven facts about missed deductions and about audit flags that your accountant won't tell you. In the Special Report…" The first eight words, in boldface type, are the most important. They tie need for this untold, secret information to an onrushing, impending event.

Direct Marketing can also *structurally* provide urgency of response. Anytime a group dynamic can be applied, a stampede effect seen, or an "act now or lose out forever" reality displayed, a higher percentage of people presented with an offer will act than will under any other circumstances. People are motivated to buy what they will not be able to get if they don't buy now, even when they would not buy now if relieved of that threat of loss. An auction is a prime example of this, and it has successfully been moved to online media—with live auctions and with timed auctions on sites like eBay. Putting people "live" into a seminar room where a persuasive speaker makes an offer from the stage, citing limited supply or discount or gift only for the first *x*-number, and *having people see the stampede* of earliest responders rushing to the product table at the back of the room, is hard to trump by any other means and impossible to perfectly replicate by any other means; however, we've learned to come close with live online webinars, where viewers can see the earliest buyers' comments, the "ticker" recording the purchase, the countdown clock for the closing of the shopping cart ticking away, and in live webinars, we can recognize by name the fast buyers. A direct-mail, fax and/or email sequence that begins by announcing that only 47 of the whatever-product will be sold (at this price, in this color, with this bonus, etc.) can, in its second piece, list the names of the first 18 buyers and show that only 29 remain, in its third piece list the names of the 34 buyers and show that only 13 remain available, and so on.

The most powerful urgency by exclusivity is having only one available. Neiman Marcus has done this for many years, in the pages of its big Christmas catalog, with unique gift items and experiences that there is only one of. For example, in one year's Christmas book, they offered a backstage experience and actual walk-on part, one night in the Broadway musical *Annie*, for just $30,000; a Woody Trailer reconfigured as an elaborate portable bar as the ultimate tailgate party vehicle, for $150,000; a private dinner for a party of 10 with a gaggle of great celebrity chefs, for $250,000; and a trip for two to Paris and Geneva, including a visit to the Van Cleef & Arpels boutique and watchmaking shop, and unique his and her watches, for $1,090,000. Will someone buy each of these one-of-a-kind gifts? Based on historical precedent with NM's annual one-of-a-kind gifts, that answer is almost certainly: yes. But, really, anybody can create one-of-a-kind gifts and experiences, or very limited availability equivalents. NM also garners an enormous amount of media attention and free publicity each year because of these extraordinary gift offers—something a local business could do at a local level just as easily.

In B2B, in the advertising, consulting, and coaching fields, this is often done with geographic area exclusivity. A collection of licensed print ads and radio and TV commercials, a seat in a mastermind group, access to various resources becomes more desirable (and can be sold for a much higher price) when only one CPA in Pittsburgh can have it; thus the race is on and any delay may put it in the hands of your arch competitor with you forever locked out.

If you look at my coaching company, Music Academy Success®, we do this for our members. Members at our

Diamond and Gold Plus levels can block out up to five competitors. Members that are Titanium level can block out actual zip codes. It's a powerful tool to have geographic block-out because there is a lot of value held in being able to keep others out of the group or opportunity.

You definitely see scarcity in my brick-and-mortar music schools, of which I own three. They are the largest schools in South Carolina, and there's absolute scarcity. We've only got so many teachers and time slots to fill, so we only accept a certain, limited number of students.

So, how could an ordinary local restaurant and sports bar create an exclusive offer with enormous inherent urgency, publicity appeal to local media, and be exciting to its customers? My prescription would be to rent a football celebrity, perhaps a local hero, and craft an afternoon and evening of activities around his presence. One offer, fairly standard: He's there for a meet 'n greet and photo opportunity during the Sunday afternoon games for any customer with autographed footballs and jerseys auctioned off during an hour within that time frame, with proceeds to a local charity…a limited number permitted in, preregistration made possible, with or without a ticket fee. Then, the exclusive offer: Just 12 patrons can buy a ticket to go into the private dining room or roped-off section, have dinner with, watch the Sunday night game with, and hang out with the star, and get an autographed ball, jersey, and photo…at, say, $52,000 per ticket. With that, there's massive urgency because there is only 12. A financial advisor, lawyer, auto dealer, etc., could utilize the same premise, renting the facility or joint-venturing with a restaurant owner, and still incorporate the local charity. The event itself would be directly profitable, reward good clients, and create new clients. The "halo effect" of the promotion to the business's entire email, social media, and mailing lists is significant, the opportunity for free but valuable publicity profound. What's most important to understand is that I took a business that is about "come on in" and eat, drink, and be merry and converted it to a Direct Marketing business, with two different, specific offers, both with created and legitimate urgency.

Another example of reinventing the business with a specific offer can be seen in the famous GIORGIO LETTERS in Dan's book *Ultimate Sales Letter* or in the Magnetic Marketing System®.

Resource Alert!

For a great offer from Magnetic Marketing, go to Page 215.

One of Dan Kennedy's friends, top direct-response copywriter John Carlton, always advises imagining your prospective customer or client as a gigantic somnambulant sloth, spread out on the couch, loath to move his sleeping bulk, phone just out of reach. Your offer must force and compel him to move now. Your goal is immediate response. A plain vanilla, dull, mundane offer just won't do it.

CHAPTER 3

Make Them OBEY ORDERS

by Darcy Juarez

Why don't we get the results we want from other people? Husbands and wives routinely complain about their spouses, expecting them to be mind readers. Managers bemoan employees' failures to perform as expected, often saying, "But I told him once." Most managers' ideas about training omit a feedback loop to ascertain comprehension and acceptance, and ignore the need for perpetual reinforcement. Everywhere you look in human-to-human communication, there is disappointment. This certainly exists for marketers, too, although many business owners don't think they should be able to outright *control* the behavior of their customers to the extent they should be able to do so with employees, vendors, or family members. In marketing and sales, control is exactly what we need. Ultimately, all of this is much about simple clarity. Do people really, clearly know what is expected of them? Or are you taking too much for granted, chalking things up as too obvious to bother clarifying?

Rule 3:
You Will Give Clear Instructions

Most people do a reasonably good job of following directions. For the most part, they stop on red and go on green, stand in the lines they're told to stand in, fill out the forms they're given to fill out, applaud when the Applause sign comes on. Most people are well-conditioned from infancy, in every environment, to do as they are told. If ever there was a mass demonstration of this, it was the years of masks, social distancing, and vaccine mandates, and wildly varied, nonsensical rules—like not being allowed to be out in the ocean, alone, on a surfboard in L.A. County or the forced closings of gyms, churches, and restaurants, but having liquor stores open. We already look back on it, a lot of us amazed at how many people followed so many orders.

There is abundant evidence that people follow directions. **Most marketers' failures and disappointments result from giving confusing directions or no directions at all.** Confused or uncertain consumers do nothing. And people rarely buy anything of consequence without being asked.

Did you know that there is a Disney Imagineer whose job is "fixing confusion"? At any spot in any of the parks where there was a noticeable slowing of movement (yes, they monitor that) or an inordinate number of guests asking employees for directions, he is tasked with figuring out the reason for the confusion and changing or creating signs, giving buildings more descriptive names, even rerouting traffic as needed to fix the confusion. This isn't just about efficient movement; it's about creating a pleasing experience. People do not like not knowing where to go or even what is expected of them.

In-store signage, QR codes in place of restaurant menus, icons on websites—everywhere you closely examine physical selling environments and media—you will find plenty of assumptions made about knowledge people have (and may not have) and plenty of opportunity for confusion. In a split-test in nonprofit fundraising by direct-mail, four different business reply envelopes were used: One was a standard prepaid business reply envelope with the standard markings. The second was the same, but with a large hand-scrawl-appearing note, "No postage stamp needed. We've paid the postage. Just drop in the mail." Third, a plain, pre-addressed envelope with an actual stamp affixed. Fourth, the plain, pre-addressed envelope with an actual stamp affixed plus the hand-scrawl-appearing note, "No postage stamp needed. We've paid the postage. Just drop in the mail." To be fair, the last two add obligation to clarity, and they were the winners by significant margin. But the first envelope was the biggest loser by a very big margin, even against the second, simply because the first presumes knowledge on the consumer's part that is not there. I got a statistically meaningful increase in conversion of visitors to buyers at a website by switching from just a "Buy Now" button to the button plus the words "Click This Button to Buy Now."

When you put together *any* marketing tool, ad, flyer, sales letter, website, phone script, etc., or *any* physical selling environment, it should be carefully examined for presumption of knowledge on the consumer's part, for lack of clarity about what is expected of them, or for wimpiness about asking clearly and directly for the desired action. Stop sending out anything without clear instructions. As an illustration, take a look at Figure 3.1 on page 49, excerpted from an actual sales letter (sent to knowledgeable buyers already in a relationship with the marketer). Note that the subhead above the copy is *quite* clear.

In my work training and coaching with Magnetic Marketing, I am constantly finding marketers giving sloppy instructions to their potential customers—or no instructions at all.

It's also worth noting that people's anxiety goes up anytime they are asked to do something but are unsure of what to expect. In Dan's book *No B.S. Guide to Marketing to Leading-Edge Boomers and Seniors*, in Chapter 15 ("The Power of Stress Reduction") he shares an example of a marketing device and copy he routinely uses with professional practices, such as chiropractic, dental or medical offices, or financial advisors' or lawyers' businesses, titled "What to Expect at Your First Appointment." Anxiety about anything uncertain grows more acute with age, but is not unique to boomers and seniors. Removing anxiety with very clear instructions, directions, descriptions, or information is a smart strategy.

The Clearer the Marching Orders, the Happier the Customer

In Direct Marketing, we have learned a lot about consumer satisfaction—which affects refunds, repeat purchases, positive or negative word-of-mouth referrals, and reviews. In every business, presented with "difficult" or complex products, many customers are quickly, profoundly unhappy. I cannot tell you the number of times I've received a product that disappointed by seeming more trouble than it's worth, and returned it or simply trashed it, and I am not alone. In direct to consumer delivery of complex products, we often add written, audio CD, DVD, and QR code directions *very clearly* labeled: Read/Listen/Scan/Watch This First. Yes, I know you will say that no one has a CD or DVD player. But they still know what a CD or DVD is. We use that with clear instructions on how they can go online to listen and watch if they prefer—somewhat like Steve Jobs used computer screen icons that look like a wastebasket and a file folder. You have to be sure that you are communicating with customers in a way that makes them feel comfortable and confident.

The Power of Good Directions

Figure 3.1 is actual "directions copy" from a sales letter, with the business identity removed. It has reinforced the scarcity/ urgency established earlier in the letter. Given phone number, times to call, and persons they'll be speaking with, an alternative drive to a website is also included. In previous campaigns, this marketer had used a much simpler instruction—essentially "Call 000-000-0000 to place your order." The copy below more than tripled the response vs. the previously used instruction.

Figure 3.1: Sales Letter

What to Do Next

Only 14 of these xxxxxxx's are available. This invitation was sent to 100 of our best customers—like you!—by Federal Express, to ensure everyone has received them at the same time and has fair opportunity to respond. Without delay. please…

Call 000-000-0000 to secure one of these 14 xxxxxxx's.
We will be accepting calls beginning at 7:00 a.m. on [Insert Date] and continuing through Noon on [Insert Next Day's Date], or until all 14 are spoken for—whichever comes first.
Helen or Rob will be available to personally take your call.

Or…

If you would like to see the xxxxxxx, a 9-minute preview video is accessible online at www.[insert-site].com. You may also instantly purchase your xxxxxxxx online, at the conclusion of the video, and receive confirmation immediately.

As always, your satisfaction is guaranteed with a 15-day inspection and return privilege. All major credit cards accepted, and the convenience of three monthly installments on request.

CHAPTER 4

No Freeloaders Allowed

By Marty Fort

Most of us try to hold people accountable for assigned tasks, but a lot of businesspeople aren't as tough on the dollars they put to work in advertising and marketing.

The economy fluctuates. There have been periods where money was running uphill. Consumers spending like the proverbial drunken sailors. At other times, for one reason or another, this kind of liquidity dries up. As I'm writing this, high inflation especially at the supermarket and the gas pump, high interest rates, wages not keeping pace with inflation, and record high credit card debt have combined to shift a lot of spending from options and luxuries to essentials. Successful entrepreneurs and savvy marketers must adapt to win in any of these conditions. One thing the tougher times do is make business owners think more carefully about their costs and about their return on investments. "Freeloaders" failing to earn their keep get evicted.

I think this is smart policy no matter if the economy is sunny or stormy. Waste of anything—a dollar, a lead, a potential customer, a customer—should not be acceptable.

This is about demanding performance.

As the leader of your business, you must do exactly that.

Rule #4
There Will Be Tracking,
Measurement, and Accountability

You are no longer going to permit *any* advertising, marketing, or selling investments to be made without direct and accurate tracking, measurement, and accountability.

You will be given all sorts of arguments against such a harsh position, by media salespeople, by online media champions talking a "new" language of "new metrics" by staff, by peers. You will smile and politely say "Rubbish." Each dollar sent out to forage must come back with more and/or must meet predetermined objectives. There will be no freeloaders; there will be no slackers.

This is now particularly vital with online and social media. Some of it is ad media pretending to be something else. Much of it wrapped in its own deliberately confusing means of evaluation—likes, views, time of views, viral, etc. It's a fact that Facebook was exposed, for misreporting and exaggerating views and numbers of minutes viewed for advertisers' videos. Widespread inflation of activity at all sites by "bots" and "fake activity farms" became known. None of this negates the use of it, but it should inform your firm insistence on clear, accurate measurements for return on invested money and time in such media, just the same as for all media. You will be told it's different, but always remember you don't get to spend different money or different hours on it. A dollar is a dollar. An hour is an hour.

There are two reasons for holding all media harshly accountable. First, because management by objectives is the only kind of management that actually works. When an NFL football team takes the field on Sunday, there are team objectives—not just winning, but for ingredients of victory—that can be measured. Each player also has individual, measurable objectives that he and his coaches have discussed before the game and will evaluate after the game. This is the way it should be when your team takes the field. Your team includes people you pay as well as marketing you pay for. You can't manage what you can't, don't, or won't measure. Vagueness must be banished.

As a season ticket holder and die-hard fan of my Carolina Panthers, I hope their coaching staff is committed to comprehensive, detailed measurement of each player's performance and accountability for performance.

I can tell you as ironclad fact that, of all our members— my clients, past and present—the richest and most successful, the ones who build the best businesses, "know their numbers" better than all the also-rans. For a full discussion of the "money math" of business, I'll refer you to Chapter 43 of the book *No B.S. Ruthless Management of People and Profits, 2nd Edition.* That book in its entirety is an excellent companion to this one, and specifically to this chapter.

The second reason for direct measurement is that you need real, hard facts and data to make good, intelligent marketing decisions. Making such decisions on what you and your employees think is happening, feel, have a sense of, etc., is stupid. And you don't want to be stupid, do you? So, let's talk about tracking response. This means collecting as much information as you can, which is useful in determining what advertising, marketing, and promotion is working and what isn't, what themes resonate with your customers and which don't, which offer is pulling and which isn't. Admittedly, this can be a bit tricky. For example, Ad #1 may pull in new customers at $123 in cost and Ad #2 at $210, so you might decide Ad #1 is the winner. But the average first six-months' purchase activity of those coming from Ad #2 is $380.00; the average from Ad #1 only $198.00. Now, which is more productive? Further, 30 percent of those from Ad #2 may refer others, while only 10 percent of those from Ad #1 refer. Now, which ad is better?

Do not dare shrug this off as too complicated. Think. Set up systems to capture the data you need and set aside time for the analysis. If it's painful and confusing at first, the fog will clear, the difficulty will abate. You will make discoveries that enable you to make better decisions, better allocate resources, create better marketing messages, and grow your business without simply growing the marketing budget proportionately. In a mature business, this is how profits can be grown without growing revenue.

There is software and there are experts in data-mining that can help with this, and they're discussed in detail in the *No B.S. Guide to Marketing Automation.** While eventually you will create complicated tracking systems, my biggest advice from this book forward is just to start with something simple, quick, and easy. One of my favorite TV shows is *Deadliest Catch*. It's about crab fishermen. These are guys that are spending millions and millions risking life and limb literally to go out and fish the Alaskan waters near the Russian border. There's a lot at stake, especially financially. But they all know their numbers and

* Available October 2024.

they can tell them to you at any time. The system they use is "the yellow legal pad system." It's a system you can use and it's super simple. When they haul in a pot of crab, the guy on the deck holds his fingers up and then the captain at the wheel, despite all of the computers around him and all the technology at his disposal, writes the number down on a yellow legal pad. Then they total it up for the day, the trip, etc. There's a lot that's instructive about that. One, that's a major reason as to why they're successful. They keep up with their crab count. They know their crab count by the day determines their entire trip. They're asking themselves—do they have to stay out longer or can they get out of the freezing snow and go inside for a bit? Have they caught enough? It determines how much longer they have to stay out there. They're using "live time data"—not getting an income statement from their accountant at the end of the quarter, when there's nothing they can do about it. They also have to keep up with government regulations. They can only go to the processors with so much crab by a certain date. They are intensely dialed in to their numbers. So, it's okay to start with just a yellow legal pad. Ask your customers how they heard about you. When they call, when they purchase, and just start tracking. Then put it in some kind of cloud vehicle, whether it's a Google Doc or something else so you can share it with your team because your staff is the second big piece of this.

Warning: Employees can often be an obstacle to accurate tracking, sometimes out of laziness, sometimes stubbornness, sometimes for more Machiavellian motives, such as concealing their own ineffectiveness. If there's been little or no tracking until now, there will naturally be resistance to the added work and to the revealed facts.

As an interesting example of what can be revealed, consider a company Dan Kennedy did some consulting for, with complex advertising and marketing bringing prospects to phone consultations. They wanted to increase the number of booked consults, but didn't know which ads or offers the consultations were coming from. When he instituted tracking on all advertising and points of data in the process, it quickly revealed not only where the customers were coming from but how effective the phone consultations actually were. The web-team was not happy with the work required to install this tracking as it created more work on their part.

Freeloaders—ads and activities and online costs that were not measurably producing consultations—were "fired." Eliminated. Marketing dollars reallocated. The company doubled revenue and nearly tripled profit year over year as a result. How much you know about what's actually happening in your business and your actions taken as a result can make a very dramatic difference.

One more example. A chain of stores with advertising that produced a lot of walk-ins had in place a process whereby the clerks were to ask everybody which ad in which media had brought them in, and stick-count it, day by day. Unfortunately, this was subject to an enormous amount of "slop." Employees didn't ask and randomly added to the count in different categories or put a lot of numbers in "Misc." A change was made, giving visitors a little survey card to fill out, pushed by huge in-store signage, entering them in a weekly drawing for good prizes—and suddenly, a lot of accurate data materialized, very contradictory to the data that had been collected or, often, just made up by the staff.

This is why it's so vital you have simple systems that are transparent, easy for anyone to understand, and are enforceable, because the more complicated they are, the more opportunities there are for people to make mistakes or hide things. I'm proud to say that I have a fantastic team managing my three music schools AND we have a robust collection of tracking methods. This gives me clear, definite facts that can't be disputed, so I can be a good coach for my team.

If you loop back and connect this to Rule #1, you'll find an important key to tracking: offers. Different offers can be made in different media, to different mailing lists, at different times. UTM parameters attached to all online links. Tracking lines tied to different offers in place of generic phone lines. Offer and promotional codes can be assigned to coupons, reply cards, surveys, online opt-in, response and order forms. Big direct-response advertisers on radio, like LifeLock and Boll & Branch, tie promotional codes to different talk radio hosts that the consumer enters at the website to secure the discount or gift, often as simple as entering the host's name. The internet also offers the local merchant an opportunity to force better tracking. Pre-internet, a local restaurant advertising on several radio shows and in a couple newspapers, giving away a free appetizer with dinner, could only try to find out which ad brought a customer in by having the customer tell the server in order to get the free appetizer, and relying on the servers to accurately stick-count and report that collected information. Now the consumer can be driven to a different, clone website to download a coupon for the free appetizer, the coupons can then be collected and tallied, and a much more accurate result obtained—plus the added benefit of capturing the names and email addresses of those visiting the site, maybe offering online reservation-making options to the consumer as well.

Tough-minded management of marketing (and of people) requires *knowing* things. Of course, hardly any tracking mechanism is perfect. The job is to get as close to perfect as you can, so that you are getting the best information possible.

Rule #5
Only No-Cost Brand-Building

I am *not* opposed to brand-building, nor would I argue against the influence, power, and value of brand. Quite a few of our Magnetic Marketing members have built powerful mainstream and niche brands, including Pro-Activ® and HealthSource (chiropractic clinics nationwide), and niche brands famous in their respective industries and fields like the Scheduling Institute (in the dental profession), American Gunsmithing Institute (with gun hobbyists), Oxbow Advisors / Ted Oakley (investment services for sellers of companies of $20 million and up), and many more. *But none of them have bought their brand recognition in the traditional way.*

My Columbia Music Academy has powerful brand identity in the Columbia, South Carolina, market. I work at getting a lot of earned (free) publicity for the schools, we do a lot of branded Direct-Response Advertising, and a huge amount of direct-mail to area parents. Because trips and events for students, giving them opportunities to perform at the Elvis mansion and theater in Memphis, Carnegie Hall in New York, and the Rock & Roll Hall of Fame in Cleveland, are a big part of my schools' added value, this earns a lot of local news coverage and even some national coverage. None of this is done just to build brand identity and name recognition. I never settle for that. Everything is tasked with creating some type of measurable response and results.

Dan Kennedy's own businesses are connected to brands. The Dan Kennedy brand is very well-known and very well-respected in entrepreneurial and marketing environments. Go google "Dan Kennedy" and see all you can find. The *No B.S.* brand attached to this very successful book series published by Entrepreneur Media also extends to the longest-running marketing and moneymaking paid subscription newsletter (the *No B.S. Marketing Letter*), and a full catalog of resources, and a membership organization. Again, none of this identity and target market brand recognition has been bought or obtained by patient and hard-to-hold accountable spending. It has all come as, essentially, a free bonus provided from direct investment only into Direct Marketing.

So, my colleagues at Magnetic Marketing and I are *not* opposed to brand-building. **We are opposed to paying for brand-building.**

Most small business owners cannot afford to properly invest in brand-building. Most start-ups lack the patient capital and luxury of time required by brand-building. I do not believe it is a wise investment for small business owners or entrepreneurs, nor do I believe it is necessary. Brand power can be acquired as a no-cost by-product of profitable Direct-Response Advertising and Direct Marketing. My preferred strategy is simple: Buy response, gratefully accept brand-building as a bonus. NEVER buy brand-building and hope for direct-response as a bonus. (Unless you are actually trying to spend daddy's fortune out of spite.)

Paying for traditional brand-building may be fine, even essential, for giant companies with giant budgets in combat for store shelf space and consumers' recognition. If you are the CEO of Heinz or Molson Coors or some company like that, playing with shareholders' money, and fighting it out as a commodity purveyor, by all means buy brand identity. But if you are an entrepreneur playing with your own marbles, beware. Copying the brand-builders can bankrupt you. You should also take note of really big, brand-name companies that are advertising brand, but also aggressively and directly asking prospects to go to a website or call a phone number, like Fisher Investments. This direct lead flow is paying for the advertising, with the contribution to brand recognition as a bonus. A relatively small percentage of brand-name advertisers know how to do this well, so you have to be very careful about who you model.

It's also worth noting that there's no guarantee of success or sustainability with widespread brand recognition and brand equity. Some once very famous and dominant brands are, today, badly tarnished shadows of their former selves, or dead. In the motel industry, the leading American brands *were* Holiday Inn and Howard Johnson's.

Pontiac was once a leading car brand in the GM portfolio, and, for a time, Rambler was the brand that stood for reliability, and Rambler dominated the station wagon category. More recently, Borders was one of the two top brands in bookselling. Some of the brands you know and perceive to be dominant leaders in their fields and product categories today will be diseased or dead within 10 years. The graveyard of once powerful brands is big, and welcomes new arrivals frequently. Any idea of inevitability of an established brand is foolish and dangerous conceit. Consider SEARS, once the Amazon of its era, and the dominant all-goods retailer, and one of the best-known and trusted brand names. None of that guaranteed its permanence.

Why, When, and How to Do Un-Branded Advertising

There is a case for ignoring branding altogether, entirely, or situationally. What I am about to reveal here is a very, very powerful advertising and marketing strategy well-known to Direct Marketers but largely ignored or misunderstood by all others. It is the deliberate use of nakedly un-branded advertising.

What you never want to do is let brand-building get in the way of the most powerful and profitable advertising and marketing opportunities to grow your business. There are many types of direct-response lead generation ads, designed to motivate qualified prospects for a particular product or service to step forward, identify themselves, and ask for information, that work much better "blind," absent any company name or logo or branding. One version is the now classic "Warning" ad:

Warning to Mutual Fund Investors:

Expert Predicts Dramatic Change and Danger in the Next 29 Days.

This Is Information You MUST Have—That Brokers Don't Want You to Know.

For Free Information and *The Wall Street Secrets Report,*

call the Fund Investor Hotline at 1-800-000-0000 or

go online to www.SecretsHotline.com.

You absolutely kill that ad's pulling power if you attach a big, fat logo, a national brand name, or a financial planning firm's name and slogan to it.

In this category, in financial and investment information publishing, one of the all-time biggest successes was a campaign that dominated print, radio, and cable TV driving traffic to an online video at EndOfAmerica.com. (You can probably still see it via YouTube.) This ad was aired, seen, and heard so much, the domain name itself nearly had brand identity, but throughout, neither the company nor its brand, the newsletter ultimately being sold, the author, or any other identity, corporate or personal, was disclosed in the advertising. It was completely "blind." I am told it broke all subscriber acquisition records of its company and probably the industry, bringing nearly 1 million new subscribers into the fold. Incidentally, as a side point, the online video was 90 minutes long, so let that stick a dagger in the persistent and erroneous beliefs about short viewer attention spans and/or the need for short copy. The point: Zero brand-building was attempted. But if in the hands of most big, dumb companies in publishing, insurance, annuities, gold, other financial goods and services, they and their nincompoop ad agencies would have insisted on mucking up the ads with their corporate names, logos, slogans, years in business.

You can always brand-build internally, with customers, once they are acquired. There's no law that says you can't create powerful brand identity and preference with customers yet never even mention it to new prospects.

There are even instances where a brand suppresses response *because of its virtues*. Dan Kennedy has had clients in niche markets who had become very well-known and well-respected leaders, and if you asked 100 people in their market about them, nearly all of the randomly chosen 100 had generally positive things to say about the company but could also rattle off the five key components of that company's sales story and offerings. No mystique, no curiosity. A been-there-heard-that-done-that-before problem. Success came by trotting out "blind" advertising and marketing with fresh promises and bold positioning, which would have been instantly discredited if voiced by the venerable, old industry leader. Then, once interest in the promises was created, information could be provided that revealed the match of the biggest, most respected brand with the hot, new, daring products.

In short, brand is not necessarily the holy grail. Brand-building is best for very, very patient marketers with very, very deep pockets filled with other peoples' money. You are likely far better served by focusing on leads, customers, sales, and profits directly driven by your marketing, letting whatever brand equity you get be provided as a free by-product of direct marketing.

Resource Alert!

Right about now, it may occur to you that the level of complexity in the multi-step, multimedia marketing and follow-up campaigns and tracking I'm suggesting is beyond your capabilities—and you may be right! But you do not need to remain hobbled; there is help to be had. There are marketing system automation experts, services, and software specifically facilitating all this for small business owners. I recommend investigating:

www.magneticmarketing.com
www.clickfunnels.com
www.magneticmarketingchallenge.com

Interview with Rick Cesari: Brand-Building by Direct Marketing

Rick Cesari is the author of a must-read book on Direct Marketing, *BUY NOW: Creative Marketing That Gets Customers to Respond to You and to Your Product,* based on his extraordinary experience bringing products like the Juiceman, the Sonic Toothbrush, and the George Foreman Grill to market.

DAN KENNEDY: Monster successes like those you've shepherded never begin that way. They begin with proving we have something to sell and proving we can craft a message that people will respond to, starting by playing small ball. I'd like you to talk a little bit about the way you started these businesses, such as the Juiceman.

RICK CESARI: We started the Juiceman business in 1989, and in three-and-a-half years we grew the sales from zero to $75 million. I found Jay Kordich, the inventor and personality of the Juiceman, at a small, local consumer show—10' x 10' booths, people selling products. All the booths had one or two people, but this one booth had a crowd, 50 people gathered. Jay was there, talking about the health benefits of juicing, demonstrating his machine, and he had people captivated. I talked with him and found out he was living on the road, working these kinds of shows, state fairs, that sort of thing all over the country, selling a lot of juice to groups. I'd already been in the direct marketing field a long time, and I was sure that we could take what he was doing on this small level, move it to media, and build it into something a lot bigger.

DAN: I think it's important I point out: Jay had a *small* business, reaching small numbers of customers, by successful direct selling. With direct marketing, you could basically multiply him with media. The reason I push owners of businesses thought of as ordinary to move away from traditional marketing to Direct Marketing is that they can multiply what they do successfully one to one into one to many with media.

RICK: That's right. But we didn't run out and make TV infomercials immediately. We made calls to get Jay booked as a guest on local radio and TV shows, to talk about health and juicing. Our first breakthrough came on a New York station, on a local morning show. Jay was on for 20 minutes and told people, if they would send in an envelope with a dollar, he'd send them healthy recipes. I was told that the station switchboard lit up, but this was before the Internet so everything happened through the mail, and it took a week before we saw the result. He was on, on June 30th. On July 6th, the mail truck pulls up, and the mailman brings in three canvas sacks. 12,000 envelopes with dollars in them. We sent out a flyer selling juicers with those recipes and that's what started this business. We used that strategy, got Jay on show after show after show. We also started using those interviews, then our first infomercial to get people to come to free health seminars, where Jay would sell from the stage to hundreds and hundreds of people at a time.

DAN: Let's be sure everybody gets that there is architecture here that does not go out of date. This doesn't have an expire date on it.

RICK: This model still works, although we get to add the Internet, we have more marketing tools—but Direct Marketing from more than 25 years ago with The Juiceman and the Direct Marketing we're applying to our latest projects *is the same*.

DAN: The next question goes to Message. Many businesspeople think that their products, services or businesses are ordinary, they complain about commoditization and competition, and they just can't see how what you've done and do, how what they see with products sold direct in infomercials, in direct-mail packages, applies to them. When you think about, basically, a blender, a countertop grill, a toothbrush, it's hard to be more ordinary than these products, yet you take them to Direct Marketing, and turn them into multi-million dollar brands, and move them successfully to retail where they sell off the shelf. Let's talk a bit about this turning the ordinary into something very saleable and very *exciting* to the public—and let me emphasize the requirement of making whatever you offer, sell, do exciting to the public. You just can't afford to accept the idea that your thing is doomed to be ordinary and uninteresting, can you?

RICK: You have to look at products *in a different way.* In 1989, there *were* a lot of juicers being sold, but they belonged to appliance manufacturers and were being sold *conventionally* as kitchen appliances. The twist we put on it with Jay was to make it a health device, not a kitchen appliance. We never talked much about the blades or motor or size of container. We pushed the information booklets, the immune strengthening diet, the weight loss juice diet, anti-aging. When we brought the Sonic Care Toothbrush out, there was one other premium priced electric toothbrush sold through dentists, but there were quite a few sold to consumers for a few dollars. Sonic Care was $150.00. How to sell a $150 toothbrush? Nobody understood or cared about sonic technology. So we made our message about reversing gum disease, preventing heart disease, etc. With the George Foreman Grill, there were a lot of little grills, and it was actually, originally a taco maker—it's slanted the way it is to slide the ground beef into the taco shell. Not surprisingly, it wasn't selling. We determined you could drain the fat and grease that way, and with George Foreman, made it about "Knock Out The Fat." Again, a health device, not just a kitchen appliance. There have been more than 30-million George Foreman Grills sold. We believe there is *always* a unique benefit.

DAN: This is one of the differences between the way most businesspeople and marketers think versus the way we direct marketers think. They look to the product and its features for benefits to talk about. We want to be storytellers. We look for the hidden benefit, for the benefit that matches up with consumers' life issues and interests.

CHAPTER 5

No Holes in the Bucket

by Darcy Juarez

I'm a Chicago girl through' n through, so the only animals I'm familiar with are "da Bears," and I haven't spent any time on farms where buckets are most commonly used. Milking cows. Carrying feed. Providing drinking water for livestock and horses. Still, it's obvious to me that doing that work with buckets full of little pinholes and leaks wouldn't be any fun or very productive.

A business is a bucket in which alchemy is to occur. Into the bucket we pour ideas, energy, work, ad dollars, marketing dollars, costs of attracting customers, costs of pursuing sales in hope of stirring into profits, maybe wealth. Most business owners are very focused on the pouring into the bucket. Few focus on exactly what happens inside the bucket. That's supposed to take care of itself. But it doesn't. It's important to have a full and accurate understanding of the investments being made. It's then important to have a strategy in place for fully and comprehensively converting those investments to the greatest possible gains.

Rule #6
There Will Be Follow-Up

Often, I find business owners with more holes in their bucket than they've got bucket! People read your ad, get your letter, see your sign, see you on Facebook, find you online, etc., they visit your website, call or visit your place of business, they ask your staff questions, and *that's it*. There's no capture of the prospect's name, physical address, email address, and no offer to immediately send an information package, free report, coupons. This is *criminal* waste. Just how much waste are you permitting to slop around in your business? Probably a lot. How leaky is your bucket? Very.

Let's talk about money you pour into the bucket. You don't just pay for the customers you get when you invest in advertising and marketing. You pay a price for *every* click, *every* website visit, *every* call, *every* walk-in. *Every one*. Doing nothing with one is just like flushing money down the toilet. To be simplistic, if you invest $1,000 in an ad campaign and get 50 phone calls, you bought each call for $20. If you're going to waste one, take a nice, crisp $20 bill, go into the bathroom, tear the bill into pieces, let the pieces flutter into the toilet, flush, and stand there and watch it go away. If you're going to do nothing with 30 of those 50 calls, stand there and do it 30 times. *Feel it*. You probably won't like how it feels. Good. Remember that feeling every time you fail—and it is failure—to *thoroughly* follow up on a lead or customer.

How to Find an Extra Million Dollars in Your Business

Could you use an extra million dollars?

If in doubt, ask your spouse or kids about it. If put to a family vote, maybe to a vote of your vendors and bill collectors, I'll wager the answer is yes. And, less facetiously, more practically, would your future benefit from getting an extra million dollars put into your 401(k) or other retirement savings account? Well, I'm happy to direct you to where that extra million is hidden inside your business. It's in the follow-up that isn't happening.

Many times, owners of profitable ad and marketing campaigns are terribly lazy about this. If they spend $1,000 to get 50 calls, only convert 5 to appointments, and only acquire 2 as customers—but worth $1,000 each—they turn $1,000 into $2,000 and are pretty happy about that. But each call cost $20, and 45 didn't turn into appointments—that's $900. Nearly as much waste as profit. But the total reality is far worse than that. If, with diligent and thorough follow-up, another 5 appointments and 2 customers could be had, he's let $900 plus $2,000 slip through holes in his bucket. If each customer can be made to refer one and an endless chain of referrals is created, the $2,900 in waste goes to $4,900, then $6,900, then $8,900, then $10,900. Let that happen once a month, it's $109,000 that should have been in the bucket that leaked out onto the floor. In 10 years, it's a million dollars. It's my experience that in just about any small business, over a 10-year term, there is at least 1 million dollars in lost money to be had. If you own a small business and would like to retire as a cash millionaire, here's your opportunity.

In most cases, the opportunity is even greater, and the possible speed of accumulating the extra wealth faster. Business owners who go from disorganized to masterfully organized at following up on leads and customers often multiply their revenues and profits, not just add to them. There are powerful tools to assist with this, like ClickFunnels (www. clickfunnels.com). Its inventor, Russell Brunson, says you are just one funnel away from a fortune. Every year, over 5,000 CF users gather, and hundreds qualify for the awards tied to their proving that promise to be true. There is a deep-dive, detailed, self-consulting approach to this from Dan Kennedy, presented in his book *Almost Alchemy: Make Any Business of Any Size Produce More with Fewer and Less,* which includes his Found Money Map. If and when you're ready to get serious about plugging every money leak in your bucket, there is help waiting for you.

This is how to use this book to make millions. Direct Marketing is never just about acquiring customers—what we call "front end." It is as much or more about retaining, repeat selling to, cross-selling to, and ascending customers on an ongoing basis—what we call "back end." It is also the means of building a system to prevent leads or prospects who could be converted to customers from getting lost and coming and going unnoticed.

Here are some of the holes in business buckets, through which money leaks:

1. **No Capture of Contact Info. As just described, this is the person who visits your website or calls and asks questions, stays unknown, and gets no follow-up.** Remember, you paid for that person. If you don't capture his contact information so you can do follow-up marketing, you wasted your money.

2. **No Follow-Up on Leads.** This is particularly wasteful. A contact-us form filled out on the website for more information that is ignored. A request for information told to "go to the website." An online chat that receives

FIG 5.1: Holes in the Bucket

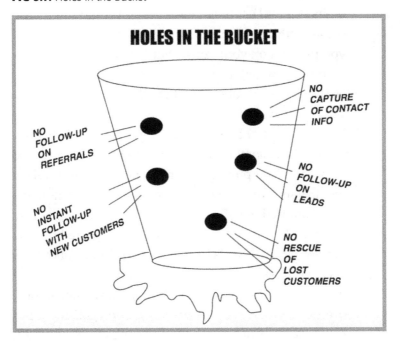

the "we are offline at the moment and will get back to you" ignored. An inbound SMS message that only receives an initial automated message. No email, no phone call, no mail, no follow-up. Nothing. Each a paid-for lead, and each opportunity wasted. The hard work was in getting the lead. Much easier to follow up than to have to go get a new lead.

3. **No Follow-Up on Referrals.** When Betty says, "I told Billy about you. I hope he gives you a call," the correct response is *not*: "Thanks, Betty. I hope he does, too." That's the common response, but it most certainly is not the correct response. You ask for and get Billy's address so you can send him a copy of your book or information package, with a note mentioning Betty's

recommendation or a note from Betty, and an offer or offers (Rule #1). If Billy fails to respond, you send him a second letter. And a third, fourth, fifth. With offers. And you put him on your newsletter list and send him your monthly newsletter. With offers. You enroll him in your six-week email "course" tied to your product or service. That's follow-up.

4. **No *Immediate* Follow-Up to New Customers.** Newly acquired customers need to become frequent and habitual repeat purchasers or ascend to higher levels of membership or somehow move from first transaction to committed relationship. This means they need to be quickly thanked, welcomed, and brought back, moved up, or otherwise committed. Think about the last five times you patronized a business for the first time—store, restaurant, service company, professional practice. What formal thank-you did you get? In four or five out of five, none. What "welcome to the family" gift did you get? None. Little or nothing was done to cement the relationship.

5. **No Prevention or Organized Rescue Efforts Related to Lost Customers.** For more than 30 years, surveys have consistently revealed "indifference by provider" as, by far, the #1 reason customers leave a business and drift elsewhere. Not some epic act of incompetence or negligence or insult, not cheaper prices, not anything major. Just a sense of indifference toward them. That left them open to easy seduction. The best answer to lost customers is, of course, not having any. That requires very frequent, very consistent, and interesting online and offline communication. But on-time rescue efforts also work. Every kind of business has a set time by which a customer should be back—for the clothing

store, it's once before each season; for the dentist it might be every six months; for the auto salesman, every three years. Whatever it is for you, alarm bells should go off for every customer not back before his stamped-on expiration date, and that alarm should set in motion a flurry of marketing and follow-up activity.

There are other holes. I've just named five. You have to find every hole in your business and plug it.

What Does No-Fail Follow-Up Look Like?

There are hundreds of variations of follow-up campaigns and strategies. One of the most reliable is structured in four main steps—although, mixing in low- and no-cost digital media like retargeting and email, each main step may have a handful of contacts, not just one. Today, you have many opportunities to create closed loops to keep reengaging prospects. Email and/ or direct mail might drive to a specific landing page housing a lead magnet or video sales letter; the viewing of that triggers a retargeting campaign, along with an email sequence and an outbound telemarketing call; a no-sale by that sequence and call triggers another predetermined sequence driving to a different landing page and video sales letter. It can all be automated. I currently have a client using five such closed loops, one after the other, each starting as the prior one ends, and, in total, encompassing 42 email contacts, 11 offline contacts, 2 online presentations, 21 phone calls, and 14 SMS messages over 11 weeks. This is all deployed with precision: Every follow-up contact is set for the fourth day, sixth day, ninth day, etc.

Here is a simplified, abbreviated look at a 4 STEPS FOLLOW-UP CAMPAIGN:

Step 1: Restate, Resell, and Extend the Same Offer

Whatever they didn't do or buy is presented to them again in the best way possible. There is acknowledgment at the start that they are getting your letter, or other communication, because they didn't buy. The message will acknowledge that there are x-number of reasons people don't respond or buy at the first appointment, visit, conversation, etc., and these reasons are then answered and made to go away. The original offer is made available, with a new deadline for response.

Step 2: Stern or Humorous "Second Notice" *Tied to Onrushing Deadline*

Classic themes and opening gambits include the good-humored, like "Are You Lost?" or "Frankly, I'm Puzzled," to the serious and stern, like "I'm Deeply Concerned about Your Failure to…" or "Are You a Man or a Mouse?" The offer is again presented, the deadline emphasized. Sometimes, the offer is slightly altered, perhaps with longer installment financing or a new or additional gift with purchase.

Step 3: "Third and Final Notice"

This ties to the deadline, and the disappearance of the offer. For a pest control company offering termite control to its route customers, this Final Notice could come from the company's attorney, in a law firm envelope, explaining that, in order to safeguard the pest control company from any liability for negligence in not fully protecting its customers' homes, it was required to clearly notify them of the hazards and costs of failing to treat a home with termite protection.

Resource Alert!
Free Book!

A great example of a good-natured sequence covering these
three steps is in Dan's book *The Ultimate Sales Letter* (4th Edition)—
the famous Giorgio Italian Restaurant letter sequence.
A Free copy of this book is available to readers at
www.UltimateSalesLetter.com/dm-book.

This has been a Direct Marketing staple for a long, long time. The very first Direct Marketer of the very first (albeit dubious) "cure" for what we now gently call ED, or erectile dysfunction, Dr. J. R. Brinkley, a turn-of-the-century promoter of goat testicle grafts to men, generated leads by radio, print advertising, direct-mail, and publicity, asked them to travel from hither and thon to his clinic, and followed up on the recalcitrant prospects with sequences exactly as described here. His marketing was so fascinating and so far ahead of its time and so remarkably effective, Chip Kessler and Dan wrote an entire book about it, rich with actual samples of Brinkley marketing gleaned from a historical society's archives: *Making Them Believe: The 21 Lost Marketing Secrets of Dr. J. R. Brinkley.*

Step 4: Change the Offer

Sometimes the offer can be altered relatively easily—by offering new or more extended installment payment terms, by swapping out a bonus for a different bonus, that sort of thing. Other times, the unconverted prospects are telling you they don't like your solution to their need, interest, or desire. That doesn't mean the need, interest, or desire is gone. Mary responded to your ad because she wanted to lose two dress sizes before her friends' annual July 4 beach party. You offered her six weeks of supervised exercise in a gym. She rejected you. She still wants to lose two dress sizes by July 4. She doesn't want to come to a gym three times a week. She might buy at-home personal training or a diet plan or pills or a gadget. Some business owners are limited to Steps #1–#3 and, as a practical matter, can't do #4. But a lot more can if they would than actually do. Trade schools began offering the option of online training for this reason. The "online university industry" is a response to the same rejection of offer but continued desire for solution with regard to post–high school education, career training, and degrees. Big direct marketers in the same interest category achieve this fourth step by swapping lead lists. People who respond, for example, to advertising about a moneymaking opportunity in real estate and stubbornly reject the offer are turned over to a marketer of a moneymaking opportunity in home-based e-commerce, in exchange for that marketer's list of prospects who have rejected his offer.

"Leave No Child Behind"

You may remember that slogan, from President Bush's administration, referring to education. Unfortunately, the problem of kids/students left behind has grown exponentially since then. Slogans don't actually solve problems.

This has, however, long been the mantra of Direct Marketers. We sometimes say "Until They Buy or Die" to answer the question: How long should follow-up be? That may be extreme, but my experience is that most business owners and marketers give up too easily and too soon on their follow-up.

CHAPTER 6

Shouting Louder Isn't Enough

by Marty Fort

P aul Revere rode through the streets ringing a bell and yelling, "The British are coming!" and everybody lit their candles or lamps and paid attention. He'd have little effect today. That was then, this is now. We are immune to noise. It's ever harder to get and hold attention just by making a lot of noise. If that worked, the marketers with the biggest bullhorns would always win and would stay on top forever, yet with increasing frequency, little upstarts unseat longevity brands and category giants. There is also the matter of message, once attention is attracted. Certainly, if you bang on my door loudly enough, persistently enough, I'll come to the door—but now, you'd damn well better have something fascinating and compelling to say.

With my music schools, I've always championed this concept. We've taken our music students to perform at the Weill Recital

Hall at Carnegie Hall, the Guest House at Graceland, and the Foster Theater at the Rock & Roll Hall of Fame. By doing so, our members and I have been featured in the nation's top print news outlets as well as numerous NBC, CBS, FOX, and ABC news affiliates. The major takeaway—offline or online, you always win by making a big noise about something, then having something genuinely exciting going on when the noise draws a crowd.

A lot of people attract a lot of attention online, on TikTok, Instagram, and other platforms. A lot of companies attract a lot of attention with big, creative, funny, expensive ad campaigns. When they draw a crowd, it often fails to turn into customers acquired and sales made because they have no marketing system to put the crowd into, and they have no clear, compelling sales message and offer for them to respond to.

Rule #7
There Will Be Strong Copy

Confronted with clutter, confusion, competition, and commoditization in the marketplace, many business owners respond by trying to shout louder. They may do this by spending more money, buying bigger ad space, advertising in certain media more frequently, hiring celebrity spokespersons or curbside clowns to wave placards. *But yelling isn't selling.*

Dan Kennedy began his business life as a salesman. Many business owners do not have such beginnings, and they are often handicapped by lack of experience with and poor attitudes about strong salesmanship. He morphed into a very successful career as a direct-response copywriter, and for the past several decades, he's been paid no less than $1 million a year to craft and write copy that sells. He knows that sales and subtlety rarely go hand in hand. Dan has often told me that he finds himself helping clients get over emotional hang-ups about this, the most common having to do with either an erroneous, often ego-driven belief that their clientele is more sophisticated than most and will not respond to "pushy" and sensational copy or a fear of what people will think of them—those people who are not customers but peers, employees, friends, family, or the public at large.

I opened my first school, just giving guitar lessons, 15 years ago. As my business has grown and become big, known, and the leader in the market, competition has grown, too. There is now a lot of competition, including low-price competitors. My chief advantage is *not* the superiority of our schools and the student experience we deliver, although that is important after obtaining customers. My chief advantage has been understanding the need for strong, exciting sales copy and specific offers.

The fact is, there is enormous, ever-growing, almost overwhelming competition for attention and interest, in every product or service category, and in general. A daily tsunami of clutter that must be cut through or circumvented. Even a numbness toward advertising, marketing, and sales messages that blocks reception in the same way driving into a dark underground tunnel blocks cell-phone reception. In this environment, the ordinary and normal are ignored, the cautious and calm messages unnoticed.

You can't send a shy, timid Casper Milktoast to knock on the door of a home or walk into a business and beg in nearly a whisper for a few minutes of the prospect's time. Send the Incredible Hulk instead—huge, glowing neon green, stomping, yelling. *He can't be ignored.* He shows up, guy drops what he's doing and pays attention. But there's a caveat…

Copy, the words in printed or online media, can't *just* shout. Loud but irrelevant isn't much better than quiet and relevant.

Loud, you can grab attention, but you can't convert it to interest. The Incredible Hulk stomping into your office would get your attention, but he'd still have trouble bridging to interest and having you engage in a conversation with him about a product or service. Would he be relevant? Credible? He'd be good for, say, cybersecurity software or services, but not appropriate for many other things. We have to be sensational and attention-commanding, but we have to do it in a way that establishes relevance and credible authority, and creates proactive interest in our information, goods, and services.

A new problem discouraging business owners from advancing their sales messages assertively and boldly, and completely, is what I'll call online and social media culture. In some social media places, overtly and assertively selling is viewed and criticized as if you showed up at church on Easter in an itsy-bitsy, teeny-weeny polka dot bikini. My advice is, first, not to be intimidated or overly concerned with how many people look at you disapprovingly as long as you are getting positive results in attracting your most desired customers and as long as you do not cross actual prohibitions of the media getting you unplugged and banished. Second, be very, very skeptical and suspicious about investing money or time in media where you are prohibited from doing what works—including delivering straightforward, powerful lead generation or sales messages.

The Four Chief Sales Copy Mistakes (That Smart Direct Marketers Do Not Make)

Most great sales copy is written backwards, from the customer's interests, desires, frustrations, fears, thoughts, feelings, and experiences, journeying to a revealing of a solution or fulfillment tied to your business. Most ineffective copy starts, instead, with the company, product, or service and its features, benefits, comparative superiority, and price. These are common default positions that the overwhelming majority of advertisers, copywriters, and salespeople fall back to, rather than developing a more creative, customer-focused positioning. With my schools, I can't start with "music lessons." I need to back up and start where the concerned, involved parent is and what they want for their son or daughter. And with the student, and why he or she is interested in music lessons. Bigger picture. Deeper meanings.

As an example, consider these two appeals to golfers:

> Now–You'll Hit the Ball Off the Tee
> Farther and Straighter
> Than You Ever Have in Your Life–
> Each and Every Time
> with "Perfect Swing"

> Or:

> Now–You'll Amaze Your Golf Buddies
> When You Hit the Ball
> Off the Tee
> Farther and Straighter
> Than You Ever Have in Your Life–
> Each and Every Time
> with "Perfect Swing"

Look closely. Only four words expressing one key customer-focused benefit.

The first headline is about two benefits. The second is about an ego-rewarding experience you'll have *because of* the benefits. We could make it even more overt and stronger:

Now–You'll Be
the Envy of
Your Amazed Golf Buddies
When You Hit the Ball
Off the Tee
Farther and Straighter
Than You Ever Have in Your Life–
Each and Every Time
with "Perfect Swing"

The first mistake is to rely on any or all of the six default positions instead of writing to and for and about the psyche of the customer.

The Six Defaults of Dumb Copywriters, Marketers & Salespeople

- About the Company

- Products & Services

- Features & Benefits

- Comparative & Incremental Claim of Superiority

- Price/Discounts

- Guarantee/Warranty

As an aside, a quick "bonus" graphics lesson: Line breaks in ad copy matter. I've carefully picked the end words and start words of each line in the above headlines, so each line is a complete idea. If I leave it up to my computer to break the lines, they end in mid-thought.

The second, closely related mistake is writing factually and "professionally" rather than emotionally, with enthusiasm, and conversationally, as you would tell somebody about your discovery. I don't care if you are selling to Fortune 1000 CEOs in sky-high boardrooms or to Papa Bear in his mobile home in the trailer park, your best approach is to write like you talk, and like you and he would talk—and to infuse your writing with enthusiasm and with deeply emotional appeals.

In the above examples, the first version had no emotional appeal. The second, the emotional appeal of greater confidence, capability, and fun; a better experience to be imagined, and the mental picture produced is of you swinging the club perfectly and watching the ball soar long and straight and true. But in the third example, that emotional appeal is secondary to the much stronger emotional appeal of doing that while observed by amazed and envious friends.

The third mistake is being timid or bland in your claims and promises. The above examples did not stop at far and straight or farther and straighter. They are bolder: farther and straighter *than you ever have in your life*. Many believe that their customers, clients, or patients are smarter and more sophisticated than others, at least immune to such sensationalism and hyperbole, possibly offended by it, and that they might be discredited if engaging in it. Such business owners are wrong. Their beliefs are in contradiction with facts. In every category of product or service, in media directed at presumably educated and sophisticated people, I can find for you a highly sensational ad making grandiose and extraordinary claims that is a huge success. Zig Ziglar was right: "Timid salesman have skinny kids"—no matter who they're selling to.

A few years back, Dan and I held two "Marty and Dan Days." Featuring individual "hot seats," so each attendee could present their burning business issue and get instant, on-the-spot advice. This carried a high ticket price. At a private lunch, after doing a number of the "hot seats," Dan said, "Marty, the trick with your school owners and a lot of business owners is they are timid." It hit me like a ton of bricks, as I knew what he was saying to be 100 percent correct. The takeaway for you is: Whatever you are timid about in your marketing efforts or your sales copy, let it go and be bigger, bolder, more dramatic. Make bigger, bolder promises.

The fourth mistake is violating Rules #1 and #2. Too much sales copy wimps out at the point of directing the reader, listener, or viewer in exactly what they are supposed to do.

Now I have some news for you that you may well consider "bad news." Many people sabotage themselves a lot by categorizing facts as either bad news or good news, rather than just as facts to be appropriately acted on. A negative attitude toward a fact makes it worse news. The fact about strong sales copy is that you need it, and you may need to learn to write it for yourself. The very small fraternity of top-level direct-response copywriters, like Dan, are in high demand and are routinely paid upwards of $15,000 to $25,000 to write copy for one ad, letter, or website, and upwards of $100,000 to write copy for a complete multi-media project, often with royalties linked to results on top of fees. They are a bargain for clients with sufficient size and scope of opportunity, but unaffordable to most of us. There is, frankly, a precipitous drop from them to a large legion of journeyman freelance writers who present themselves as copywriters but often have little or no Direct Marketing experience or acumen.

Most small businesspeople who have strong copy in their marketing learn to write that copy for themselves. If this happens to be brand new to you, start with Dan's book *The Ultimate Sales Letter (4th Edition)*, his *Magnetic Marketing System®*, and the Offer on Page 215. The good news is, you will quickly see, by comparing the examples given here in this book, and the examples in these recommended books and resources, where and how your copy is weak and how you can strengthen it—in many cases with minor yet significant changes, just as seen here with the golf example.

You CAN learn to write strong sales copy. I did, with no background in it. Today, not only am I the chief copywriter for my schools, but my advertising and marketing is licensed to and used by hundreds of schools.

CHAPTER 7

Tux, Tails, & Top Hat or Coveralls & Work Boots?

by Darcy Juarez

A lot of Direct-Response Advertising is *ugly*—on purpose. Plain. Featuring a lot of text, seemingly squeezed in, often in small print.

Businesspeople like fancy advertising. They like to dress up their advertising and marketing, in professional or elegant attire, and they are easily persuaded to do so by agencies and media. Business owners love hearing praise for the cleverness, cuteness, or comedy of their marketing. Their egos are not concerned with results, but with feeling good and proud. They want to display their logo and their slogan.

As Direct Marketers, we are not concerned with any of that. We prefer work clothes. We're not dressing up our marketing for approval by snobs at the fancy dress ball. We're getting its sleeves rolled up, its work boots on, and ready to do a job.

Rule #8
It Will Look Like Mail-Order Advertising

In the last chapter, copy. Next, appearance. Fortunately, Direct Marketing revolves around only a short list of Rules presented here, and Direct-Response Advertising revolves around an even shorter list of choices of formats. It is to look a certain way.

This is going to shock many of you to your core. It can, if you let it, simplify your life and make you a great deal of money. This Rule is a great simplifier, because it ends your paying attention to—and trying to emulate—the overwhelming majority of all the advertising you see on TV, in magazines, in newspapers, online; by your peers and competitors. You are to go blind to anything except *pure* mail-order advertising, which I'll tell you how to identify, and where to find, to observe, in a minute. But first, this is very important: All advertising except mail-order advertising will, from here on out, be willfully ignored. You will resist any temptation whatsoever to borrow from any of it, copycat any of it, worry about differences between it and your approach. You will, in fact, live in utter defiance of its norms.

I am specifically speaking of the formats, layout, and appearance of advertising—whether a print ad or a website or any other item. Classic mail-order ads are typically broken up into one-fourth, one-half, and one-fourth of the page, give or take. The top quarter is for headline and subheads, the middle half for presentation of product or proposition, sometimes aided by testimonials, and the bottom quarter is for the offer and clear response instructions, often with a coupon. The most frequently used alternative is the advertorial, which mimics an article. If you will stick with these two formats, you can safely ignore all others. The pay-per-click ad mimics the classified ad. The home page of a website mimics the classic ad: There is a headline and subheads at the top, some product or proposition info in the middle, and a click to order, a form to fill in, an email box to fill in, at the bottom. This may be assisted with video. It may *not* be polluted with top, side, or bottom panels offering a myriad of click options taking visitors hither and thon and putting them in control of an experience full of variables. It will be the start of a single, focused sales presentation leading to a decision, response, or purchase instructions, and an action— just like a print ad.

The other reliable format is that of a letter, from you to the reader, at whatever length is needed to do the job. We mail 4-, 8-, 16-, 24-, and in one case 64-page sales letters. One of these, the 16-page one, literally tacked up online as a landing page, having traffic driven to it, produced over $1 million a year for 9 years' running.

To see real mail-order advertising, you need to assemble a diverse assortment of magazines in which many highly successful mail-order companies consistently run full-page advertisements. These include *Reader's Digest Large Print Edition*, Farm Bureau journals, tabloids like *National Enquirer*, business publications like *Investor's Business Daily*, *Entrepreneur*, and *Forbes*. Almost all special interest magazines for model railroad hobbyists, gun enthusiasts, horse lovers, etc., have fractional and full-page mail-order ads. You can find them all at a Barnes & Noble newsstand or at your public library. The response mechanism in these ads won't, in most cases, be mailing in a coupon, but instead calling an 800 number or going to a website; otherwise, the ad might have run in 1950 and will probably be doing fine in 2040. You will also encounter advertorials in the same publications. Tear out and keep these ads, and *discard all others*. Let these true mail-order ads be your only models. If you will respond to some, your mailbox will soon be full of direct-mail, also following classic formats and architecture.

Resource Alert!

We feature this kind of advertising for diverse businesses
in most issues of the *No B.S. Marketing Letter.*
See Page 215 for your opportunity to receive it.

I also want you to seek out—Google, Amazon, etc.—the following legendary mail-order men: Joe Sugarman, Gerardo Joffe, and E. Joseph Cossman. Get their books. Study their ads. These men know how to format a mail-order ad.

As you come to recognize the main mail-order ad formats (and everything else that isn't), you should build what direct marketing pros call "swipe files" for yourself, filled with sample ads torn from different magazines and newspapers, downloaded from the web, retained from mailings—only the mail-order style ads. When you go to create something for yourself, you can review these samples for inspiration, ideas, and to keep you inside the guardrails of mail-order ad appearance. **Understand, what I am telling you to do is "strange."** On its surface, it is akin to telling you to put your car in storage and drive a boat to and from work on city streets. Others who see you using mail-order ad formats for your business will think you as batty as if you were driving a boat down the highway. That's okay. There's method to the madness

First, only mail-order ads actually persuade people to buy things and to do so immediately and directly. Presuming you would like to sell things with your ads, I suggest it's not *really* strange at all to emulate only the ads that sell, rather than emulating all kinds of ads that do not sell. Other ad formats and styles may brand-build, please the eye aesthetically, be praised as creative, win critical acclaim and awards, affect market share over time, immeasurably and uncertainly influence, plant thoughts that later influence purchasing. But only mail-order ads sell and sell now. For you this may mean "selling" free information, a visit to a retail location, an exam or diagnostic call, viewing an online presentation, attending a webinar, or an actual product or service. In ANY case, you want to make a sale; to get an immediate response, so copying mail-order advertising is the most relevant.

Think about it this way: If you wanted to succeed as a salesperson in a given field, and there were disdained but highly successful and prosperous salespeople and there was a much larger, more peer-popular, more commonly seen group of salespeople suffering from elongated sales cycles, poor conversion rates, barely eking out a living while hoping to build up goodwill that will pay off someday—which ones would you want to be permitted to shadow for a few weeks, then emulate? Mail-order advertisers, offline and online, are the first group. Most of the advertising you see is from the second. Beware. Be wary. Be smart!

Second, sticking with mail-order ad formats prohibits a lot of mistakes. Dan has also written two fiction books, and the advice he got when he was writing the first book was from a published novelist who was kicking out new books in three different series every six months. She said she always put her characters only in places she knew well, confined herself to plots she used repetitively, and basically operated within a small box. The same is true for the business owner or entrepreneur who is somewhat the amateur at Direct-Response Advertising. If you let yourself roam outside a small box, you are vulnerable to being led astray in a dozen different directions, to winding up with "cool" and creative websites and ads that don't sell. You have three boxes: the classic, pictorial mail-order ad, the advertorial, and the letter. Stay inside those three boxes.

As encouragement, let me show you a very simple and straightforward example of mail order–style advertising for an ordinary, local business: landscaping. If you made a point of finding all the newspaper, magazine, direct-mail, and online advertising from the landscapers in your area, it's unlikely any would look like this one. Instead, they'd be full of photos, illustrations, the company names, logos, lists of services, and would look like a professionally prepared ad, like all other ads—a guy in a black tuxedo amid a lot of other guys in black tuxedos at a wedding reception or charity ball. A bunch of penguins. This ad is the lone guy who wandered in, in a plaid flannel shirt, denim coveralls, and work boots. Can't miss him.

Figure 7.1: Article Reprinted from the *No B.S. Marketing Letter*

Dan Kennedy's

MILLION DOLLAR MARKETING LESSON
Class is in session. The Professor of Harsh Reality and Grand Opportunity is here.

My Platinum Member Mike McGroaty wears denim coveralls, says "aw shucks", and plays at being "just a dumb dirt farmer." He is anything but. He has built and runs a successful farm, nursery and landscaping business, and has a thriving info-business, teaching "backyard nursery operation" to hobbyists and home-based businesspeople, for fun 'n profit. Here is an inspirational lesson in direct marketing that every local bricks-n-mortar or service business owner can profit from....

The Million Dollar Lesson, in Mike's own words:

"Dan, I recently ran this ad to see if it still worked – I haven't used it *since 1996* **(EXHIBIT #2)**. I guess I wanted to prove to the local Chapter/Mastermind Members that simple, straight-talk ads like this still work – I see them struggling with cluttered ads that won't produce and a lot of time-sucking online activity they can't measure. I ran this – again, RECENTLY – in a local, community newspaper, with about 50,000 circulation, for $400.00. It's written to repel more than it attracts. Those who can't spend $2,000 don't call. Those who live in $300,000 or $400,000 'mansions' don't call. Its target is the retired blue collar folks, in modest homes, in the working class neighborhoods, age 57 and up. 14 people called and we did 2 jobs. (We video taped one and I'm now going to make a how-to product out of this. Most of these re-landscape jobs can be done in under 6 hours with 3 guys, and the operator can net about $900.00 As you say, no reason to be broke in America.)

The history of this ad goes back to 1983, when I was tired of working for really arrogant people with money AND I was broke. I wanted quick, easy jobs that I could do in one day, not over three weeks. I started with a small ad (shown on page 69 of my book*) and it worked. I ran it in a coupon book 6 times a year *for 13 years*, with a 20-1 ROI. I went to the library to learn WHY it worked and found the book 'Tested

Advertising Methods', and I've been a student of marketing ever since. This ad is an expansion of the original, and as I just proved, it, and the old-fashioned newspaper, still work just fine.

[*Mike's book, *Can Any Small Business Make You Rich?* Is available at TurnTheCrankMarketing.com. You should read it. If you have a "young entrepreneur and future millionaire" in the family, it's great for him or her too.]

By the way, the Mailbox Million Training, great stuff. My biggest takeaways haven't sunk in yet, but the one thing that resonated with me was: 'you can sell people things they AREN'T searching for.' In my info-marketing business, hardly anybody goes online searching for what we sell, but when you said it at Mailbox Millions, it really hit home. Also, that I need to focus on the 5% who will pay more and the 1% who will pay a lot more. With 100 new customers a week, we are leaving a lot of money on the table. "

Now, a caveat. This ad operates in contradiction to Ben Glass' advice elsewhere in this issue of The No B.S. Marketing Letter, where he says "the purpose of your ad should not be to make a sale. That's making the ad do too much work." Ben advocates lead generation and follow-up by media (not manual labor), to lead to the sale – also the approach I usually prefer and champion. Ah, but, there is more than one way to be right. And marketing choices are situational, not universal or absolute. Technically, even Mike's ad is lead generation, with a free offer (for estimate and design), but Mike also has his ad doing a lot of heavy lifting, nearly making the sale, disclosing price. This is why we test different approaches, and show you different approaches, so you can get to a customized 'ultimate marketing plan' that perfectly suits you. Ben is one of the smartest professional practice marketers there is on Planet Dan or anywhere else, but he and I and everyone else must be used as guides, not dictators.

■■■■■

Figure 7.2: Ad Reprinted from the *No B.S. Marketing Letter*

Your House Re-Landscaped only $1,995!

Just look at everything you get for this crazy low price!

First of all, the consultation, the estimate and the design are free. You won't pay a dime unless you hire me to actually do the work. I will design a landscape that not only compliments the architecture of your home, but a landscape that is pleasing, colorful, interesting, and very, very easy to care for. This design will include an array of beautiful plants, all hand selected at the nursery by me. I'll show you photos of the plants that I am proposing for your home and I will give you a written, signed estimate.

If you hire me to do the work this is what you can expect to happen:

We'll come out and rip out all of the old shrubbery in front of your house and haul it away. I will personally layout the planting beds with a gentle design of sweeping curves that will be attractive and very easy to navigate with a lawn mower.

All weeds and grasses will be removed.

We'll then wheelbarrow by hand, (no machines tearing up your lawn!) a minimum of five cubic yards of good, rich topsoil into the planting beds.

Once the planting beds are prepared the new plants will be brought in and very carefully arranged before they are installed, making sure each plant is precisely placed in the landscape. Once planted I personally do any pruning that is necessary so the finished landscape looks great and you won't have to touch it all summer!

We'll finish up by applying two to three inches of hardwood bark mulch and then I've got a secret weed control strategy that works incredibly well to keep your new landscape weed free for many months to come.

That's it! You don't have to lift a finger. The most work you'll do is picking up the phone to call.

When we are completely finished we'll clean up and make sure there is nothing left for you to do. As I mentioned earlier we haul away all of the debris.

That's what you get for $1,995.

Wait! That's not all.

You also get a no questions ask one year guarantee on every single plant. That's right, if you lose any plants in the first twelve months I'll come out and replace them free of charge! Seriously. All of the plants are guaranteed to live for one full year.

There are a couple of other things you should know. One, I'll be on the job working right along with my crew. I am not going to send a bunch of unsupervised knuckleheads to your house. I just won't do that!

I'll be there with my son Duston. Duston has been working with me for years and he knows as much about this as I do. We'll probably bring somebody else along as well to help with some of the heavy work.

As much as I love doing these re-landscape jobs, they are a lot of work and as much as I hate to admit it, swinging a spade, a spud bar, and pushing a wheelbarrow all day kick my baby boomer butt! I need a lot more breaks than I used to that's for sure!

But I truly enjoy doing these re-landscape jobs, I love the people I work for, and I love the look on their faces when the jobs are done.

The other thing that you should know is that we don't mess around. We are not going to come to your house, make a mess then disappear for days or weeks at a time. Once we start we stick with it until it's done unless the weather forces us to postpone for a day. But won't leave you with a mess. We'll get in, get it done and get out!

You will be very, very pleased when we are done. I promise!

Okay, now here's the catch. I've only got time to do a few of these re-landscapes. I might do three of them, maybe four, absolutely no more than five. If you're interested I suggest you call right now.

Remember, there's no obligation, the estimate and design are free.

Michael J. McGroarty
McGroarty Enterprises Inc.
Perry, Ohio 44081
440-223-5309

P.S. I really am only going to do a few of these. Wish I could do more, but you know ... Time is the elusive monster.

CHAPTER 8

Money in the Bank

by Marty Fort

In any and every business, you're actually in a number of businesses. Most businesses have many deliverables, not one. A dental practice may be in the teenage teeth-straightening business with products from traditional braces to Invisalign®, but also in the implant business with seniors. Each business is the same. A quantum leap in income occurs when an entrepreneur differentiates deliverables from business, and sees himself in the marketing business. An even more profound shift in thinking takes us to *being in the money business*. It is possible to be in business for reasons other than money, but it's rarely a good idea, and it's usually more accurate to term such endeavors hobbies and tax losses. Most business owners are, above all else, acknowledged or not, in the money business. There is a relationship between your acceptance of that fact and behaving accordingly and the amount of money you make. When you fully grasp that you are in the money business, you think, behave, and govern differently than when you think you are in some other business—and your income automatically improves.

There are harsh realities in business. Business is about profit. Who and what makes a satisfactory contribution to profit belongs in the business. People and things that do not, don't.

Rule #9
Results Rule. Period.

Consider the simple agreement: You want your car hand-washed and waxed outside, vacuumed out inside, for which you will pay your neighbor's teen $20. If he does not wash or wax or vacuum the car but wants the $20 anyway, what possible "story" could he offer in place of the result of a clean car that would satisfy you? I would hope none. You didn't offer to pay for a story. You offered to pay for a clean car. The same is true with advertising and marketing investments, and do not let anyone confuse, bamboozle, or convince you otherwise.

Further, no *opinions* count—not even yours. Only results matter.

One of the best things about Direct-Response Advertising is that we can run split-tests and tests against controls. If I have two ideas for positioning and promoting the same product or place of business—let's say one has to do with the organic and health benefits of the food, the other with the gourmet and exotic nature of it, the "cool" factor—I can create two ads or just two different headlines for the same ad, and test them in the same environment. On the internet, I can use Google and SEO to drive traffic to two different landing pages. Offline, I might split a mailing list in half. I might put a free-standing insert about idea #1 in half a day's newspapers, and FSI about idea #2 in the other half. By adhering to Rule #4, I will then *know* which produces more and a better response. I don't have to settle for anything less than *knowing*. That's a split-test. If you have an ad, an Every Door Direct Mail piece, a postcard, a website, anything that works satisfactorily, in direct marketing industry lingo, you have a control. We test one variable at a time against that control, in split-tests. Again and again and again, as often and as cheaply as we can. When a change boosts response, it is incorporated into a new control.

By these means, we arrive at a definite factual conclusion provided by actual results. This negates any and all opinions. Results rule.

One of the biggest direct-response advertisers in financial services, offering credit cards and loans to small businesses and to consumers, reportedly conducted over 10,000 split-tests and tests against controls in one year's time. That is a big commitment to smart, scientific, sophisticated Direct Marketing!

If you operate a very small business and can't figure out how to do much of this kind of testing, then the next best thing is to pay very, very close attention to national direct marketers selling comparable ideas, goods, or services to your customers, because they are doing a lot of testing, and their controls are visible. If, for example, you are a doctor or a hospital, you would pay very close attention to the health and alternative health newsletter publishers and the nutritional supplement companies who market by direct-mail, radio, TV, and online—and it is easy to get on all these mailing lists and get all their mail; just subscribe and buy from a few. Use different versions of your name (John Smith, John A. Smith, J. A. Smith, etc.) and different addresses (your office, your home, your parents') so you get multiple copies of the same mailings and can more easily determine that a particular piece is being mailed expansively, often, and repetitively over months, marking it as a control. Emulate people like Brian Kurtz, who in the decades he directed the marketing at Bottom Line Health, Bottom Line Personal, and Boardroom sold millions of dollars of health-related "cure" books and newsletters by direct-mail, spent tens of millions of dollars mailing their sales materials, and ran umpteen split-tests and tests against controls. This hugely successful company continues to develop, test, refine, and mail millions of such pieces every year. Their test results can be yours to use. The same thing exists in almost every product, service, need, interest, or subject matter category. There *are* direct marketing leaders selling to *your* customers. Study them.

Back to health: If five different smart direct marketers' controls all feature, as a bonus with purchase, a book, report, or CD about remedies for joint pain—even though some are selling books, others newsletters, others pills, and none are selling a joint pain remedy—and they are mailing to consumers ages 50 to 70, and you have any kind of a local health practice and want to attract patients ages 50 to 70, and you fail to create and offer as a gift a book, report, or CD about remedies for joint pain, you are a blockhead.

If you can combine leveraging other marketers' test results by studying and extracting common success factors from their controls with your own testing, you can develop "killer" promotions, campaigns, marketing materials, websites, and web videos. Yes, I'm afraid this requires you to become a serious student, observer, and analyst of top direct marketers successfully selling to your customers and prospects. Yes, it requires you to actually work to elevate your game. No, there's no one magic app for this. But if you sincerely want to raise yourself out of the clutter and above your competition, this IS the work you will do—because I can promise you, they won't.

A lot of my success is frankly due to the fact that I outwork other people. Whether it's putting in long days for Magnetic

Marketing, ClickFunnels, or my own companies, I'm here to do the work. I also delegate through an awesome team of almost 100 people that help me free up my time and bandwidth. That creates "Time Wealth." I enjoy a lot of time wealth, by paying people well and creating great companies. But to get them off of the ground, I do work hard to elevate my game. Dan said to me years ago in a meeting, "Marty, you get the 'Get S**T done award.'" By this point, I should be an annual recipient. You can call it TCB (Taking Care of Business) as Elvis and the Memphis Mafia would.

It's Going to Get Weird—Embrace the Weirdness

A lot of what you see and are told throughout this book, and that you'll discover if you begin collecting, accumulating, and studying major direct marketers' direct-mail and other marketing, will look, sound, or feel *wrong* to you. Too bold, too aggressive, too hype-y, too unprofessional, too weird, too contradictory to everything you see done in your field. Of course, that's the old you reacting to it, before you became a knowledgeable Direct Marketing pro. Regardless, your opinion *never* counts. You don't get a vote, because you don't put money into your cash register. Your spouse, momma, neighbor, golfing buddy, competitor, or employees don't get to vote either, for the same reason—and you must explain to them, in no uncertain terms, that they have no vote. The clout belongs exclusively to the customer. The only votes that get counted are the customers', and the only legal, valid ballots are cash, checks, and credit cards. Everything else is B.S.

With this Rule #9 to live by, you will be the most results-oriented businessperson on the planet, immune to opinion, criticism, or guesswork. If it sells, it's good. If it doesn't, it isn't. You are going to quickly become "Mr. or Mrs. or Miss Money in the Bank." If you can't clearly track money in the bank from something, stop doing it. There's likely an EXIT sign above a door in your place of business. Through that door goes anything and everything (and anyone) not definitively putting money in the bank. And if something that does put money in the bank is "weird," so be it.

Tim Ferris says he chose his first book's title, *The 4-Hour Workweek*, by testing many possible titles via Google. The winning title was not his preferred choice. He let the market choose. His book soared to best-seller status and made him famous and rich.

Dan Kennedy had a client with upscale home furnishings stores who suffered a wife thoroughly embarrassed by his personality-driven, inelegant direct-mail campaigns. Every year he spent a good-sized sum producing a fancy, slick, prestigious brochure about his stores that he never actually used. The entire exercise was to give his wife something she was willing to let her family and friends see, that represented their business! Many people have echoed her level of distress to me about using Direct-Response Advertising—until they saw and banked the results.

To be a committed Direct Marketer, you must be committed to *results*.

The world, incidentally, is overrun with people claiming a desire for all sorts of results—from wealth to weight loss—but unwilling to do what is required to achieve the results, even when that requirement is clear and within their doing. That is a fundamental difference between the few winners and the bulk of losers in every endeavor: The winners prize the desired result above every other consideration and are willing to do whatever it takes (within the law) to get that result. The losers think and say they want the result, but they want it only if they can have it somehow gifted to them, without meeting its requirements.

When it comes to driving a business to exceptional heights, an income to the top 5 percent or 1 percent, a product to dominance in the marketplace, there are known requirements—almost always including violating industry norms, being judged odd and being roundly criticized, setting aside all opinions, and relentlessly focusing on what works.

CHAPTER 9

No Chocolate
Cake for You!

by Darcy Juarez

einfeld's creation, The Soup Nazi, was a memorable character. The proprietor of a soup shop, told anyone who annoyed him, "No soup for you!" If you're going to get very far with this conversion to Direct Marketing, you're going to have to yell at yourself and deny yourself things you've been indulging in. By the time you finish this book, you'll have seen the prior nine Rules applied and been directed to a number of places where you can see them applied. What may have started as mysterious will be understood. You'll be able to spot Direct Marketing when you see it. You'll know what needs to be done. The real question left will be about your will to do what you know needs to be done.

Rule 10
You Will Be a Tough-Minded Disciplinarian and Put Your Business on a Strict Direct Marketing Diet

I'm afraid I've been on my share of diets. I've been unable to make myself *like* any of them. We want to eat what we want to eat. In my Chicago, *we eat*. Deep dish pizza. Lasagna. Subs. Comfort foods. We have big family dinners. Sticking to a diet isn't easy.

I know that what I'm going to demand of you—sticking to a strict Direct Marketing Diet—isn't going to be easy either.

Business success is, in many ways, about doing difficult things. Many business owners who perennially struggle and suffer are very much aware of things that need doing but simply lack the will to do them. There's a longtime employee or vendor or client, now a "friend" who you know is toxic and detrimental and needs to be replaced, but you can't muster the will to fire them. There's advertising you keep spending money on that you know is failing to produce measurable results, but you lack the will to end it or fix it. There's that website you know isn't producing either, but the very thought of getting it remade (yet again) is painful, so it stays as is.

The will to win is found in winners and is often absent in also-rans. This is a consistent theme of success—broadly, and narrowed to marketing. In Napoleon Hill's classic book *Think and Grow Rich*, Hill identified what he called *"burning desire."* Not mere, run-of-the-mill, gee, it'd be nice to have "x" kind of desire. Burning. Years later in sports, legendary Vince Lombardi spoke often about the will to win. He acknowledged that the talent and skill of players on a team, the brilliance of the game strategy and coaching, and even luck all paled as success factors when measured against the will to win. If you dig into the biographies and authoritative works about Steve Jobs, Jeff Bezos, and others equivalent to the men Hill studied in his time, you cannot avoid the fact of obsessive will to win and willingness to do what is necessary to win

With advertising and marketing, you have to be thick-skinned toward criticism, tough-minded about money invested, extremely disciplined in thought and action, and adherent to a winning game plan, all fueled by a resolute will to win.

If you go on a diet—*seriously*—there are some things you need to do. First, purge your refrigerator and cupboards of fattening and junk foods. And keep them free of them. Celery sticks, not cookies. Second, decide on an eating plan and stick to it patiently and persistently. Make it simple, with hard and fast rules you can remember. For example, not eating anything white is a very simple rule to remember. Third, get some tools, like a scale. Fourth, count something—calories, fat grams, carbs, WW points, *something*—so you can manage with numbers. Fifth, step up your exercise. Finally, sixth, be very alert to hazards and scams that lead you astray. As an example, a friend recently, proudly showed me the bottle of "Vitamin Water" she had switched to from soda pop to be healthier. The label on the small bottle of red gunk said it was a delivery system for *32 grams of sugar*! Gotta read the labels—if you're serious.

Same thing with your transformation to a lean, mean Direct Marketer.

First, purge your business of junk, like fancy websites that violate most of the previous nine rules. Dead image or brand ads that just lay there. Gentle, subtle, plain vanilla sales letters. Media that can't be ruthlessly measured and held accountable. Uncooperative staff. Out with the old, in with the new. Not slowly or gradually either. Just like with the refrigerator and pantry—get a big trash bag and purge. The great success philosopher, Jim Rohn, was known far and wide for preaching the gospel of Massive Action. Key word: *massive*. This is what Dan, Marty, and I want this book to inspire you to do, and give you the gumption to do: take massive action and install Direct Marketing.

Second, decide on a new marketing plan. Like the eating plan, it's best if it is simple, with hard and fast rules that are easy to remember. Rules #2, #3, and #4 are just as clear, simple, and easily kept in mind as Eat Nothing White.

Resource Alert!
Free Book!

Dan's book The *Ultimate Marketing Plan (4th Edition)* is a good guide to creating your own simple and straightforward marketing plan. Get a free copy of both *The Ultimate Marketing Plan* and *The Ultimate Sales Letter* by going to www.UltimateSalesLetter.com/dm-book.

Third, get some good tools. New ads, flyers, sales letters, websites, email follow-up sequences, social media content, scripts for handling incoming calls, and maybe marketing system software like ClickFunnels, which powers Magnetic Marketing, and many of our Members' businesses. The best "getting started toolkit" is included with the Most Incredible Free Gift Ever offered at the end of this book, and includes some of the best videos and trainings from Dan Kennedy.

Fourth, start counting and measuring things. Closely monitor numbers that matter.

If you don't come up with things you can count and measure by hour, day, week, month, and ways to hold every dollar invested directly accountable, your attempt at conversion from ordinary marketing to Direct Marketing will fail.

Fifth, step up your exercise—to build your marketing-mind muscle. Throughout this book, we recommend other books; Dan's and others. If you're like most business owners you get completely caught up in the "doing of things," to such an extent that you aren't actually thinking much, let alone considering new and different and potentially better ways of growing your business. These days, this has escalated to new mental illness, as people have removed even the minutes of walks from business to car or with the dog from thinking time to texting time and email checking time and social media updating time. I suggest at least one hour first thing in the morning and one hour in the evening given to reading success literature and marketing information, and making notes and working on changes and improvements in your business. Further, you need to actually become your business's CMO— chief marketing officer—and devote a significant amount of time just to marketing work. Professional practice owners can force all their appointments into four days and block one day a week to do marketing work and only marketing work. Others can start one hour earlier each day, beginning with one solid hour of marketing work before starting the day. You also need to mentally exercise and build marketing-mind muscle by association with other businesspeople committed to Direct Marketing, in your category of products and services if possible, or/and in diverse businesses.

Sixth, finally, be alert for and resistant to those who would dissuade or distract you from putting your business on the Direct Marketing Diet. You need to be very careful not to let anything into your new Direct Marketing business that doesn't belong there. I have a friend who knew that cookies were her downfall. No cookies ever allowed in the house. If they make it home from the store, they are put in the outside garbage can, watered down to mush, with more garbage thrown on top. Why? Because if they make it into the house, she doesn't have the discipline to say no. So she can't let it in. You've got to do the same thing with your business. Anything that doesn't conform to the Rules here, do not let in at all. Just say no. And bar the door.

There will be a time when you have done such a great job with the Direct Marketing Diet that you can loosen up a bit. Indulge some of your own creativity. Violate one of the Rules for good reason. At the beginning, though, you will get the best results, by far, by sticking to the Diet.

CHAPTER 10

The Results Triangle

by Dan Kennedy

Every Direct Marketing system I've ever devised for any client—and they now number in the thousands, commanding fees exceeding $100,000 plus royalties—every one has been based on this Triangle. It is not, therefore, unique to this book. I teach it elsewhere, often, and rely on it as I do gravity and oxygen.

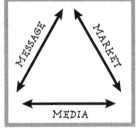

There are basically three components to marketing, for anything, anywhere, at any price, to anyone. Every individual loves to insist his business circumstances are somehow different. Not so. Every business, past or present, requires these three things to prosper: a marketing Message, a Media to deliver it, and a receptive Market affordably reached, to respond to it. These three cannot be placed in any certain sequential order, because no single one is more important than the other, and none can function without the others. It is a closed triangle. Each feeds the others. If you will, "marketing energy" flows to and from each component, from each one to the other two.

There are a number of ways to render the Triangle powerless:

Right Message → **Wrong Market** → Right Media

Right Message → Right Market → **Wrong Media**

Right Message → **Wrong Market** → **Wrong Media**

Wrong Message → Right Market → Right Media

Wrong Message → **Wrong Market** → Right Media

Wrong Message → Right Market → **Wrong Media**

Wrong Message → **Wrong Market** → **Wrong Media (the trifecta)**

There's only one way to get it right.

Right Message → Right Market → Right Media

Now let's look at getting all three parts functioning effectively and in sync with the others.

Markets
How to Discriminate for Fun & Profit!

With a nod to Dr. Seuss, the WHO is very, very important.

When you choose and use Media, it's vital to know WHO you are trying to reach, attract, interest, and persuade, and how they prefer to be offered and receive information and offers. When you craft your Message, you need to know WHO it is for (and WHO it isn't). **The WHO you want as a customer gets to govern** *everything.*

If you reread that paragraph, you'll think it all obvious. Yet, most marketing remains product centric, not customer centric, and most marketing is very broad and vague and generic, not narrow focused and specific. If you consider non-Direct-Response Advertising—i.e., image or brand advertising—its emphasis is on the company and the brand, not about the customer.

Most small businesses attempt to influence the ocean with thimbles-full of water. When you have comparatively limited resources, you must deploy them very selectively.

Sadly, most businesspeople cannot accurately and completely describe exactly WHO they want to respond, WHO is their ideal customer, WHO is their current customer, and for the most part they are playing Blind Archery. A dangerous game.

I have dealt with many, many, many examples of this over the years. Let me tell you about three that are instructive and, in very, very different businesses, reveal the same very powerful, profitable, pretty much secret principle.

Scenario #1: A member of one of my coaching groups owned a very profitable, very unusual business: For a fee, his company helped frustrated U.S. men meet and marry brides from foreign countries and arrange for their immigration. His was a one-stop-shop, providing access to thousands of women in Russia, Asia, and other lands eager to marry U.S. men, who had been pre-screened, facilitated communication, coaching, trips to the different countries, and assistance with legal matters. The basic fees were $495 to $995 when he joined my group, but they quickly leapt to $4,995 to $9,995 on my advice, with no change in client acceptance, although that's not my point here. I questioned him about the WHO of his business. Who were the clients? Who were the *best* clients? He told me they were everybody: preachers, teachers, truck drivers, pro golfers, executives, barbers, butchers, and candlestick makers. But when I asked if there were more of one than the other, I hit the nerve; he didn't know. So we investigated. And we found that about half of all the clients were twice-divorced, long-haul truck drivers. Now I want you to think about what use we might make of that piece of information, and we'll return to it a bit later.

Scenario #2: A client sold a home-based business opportunity aimed at "white collar" men and women. He advertised in *USA TODAY*, newspapers, and business opportunity–type magazines, like this book's publisher's magazine, *Entrepreneur*. Again, I inquired about the WHO. His buyers included "all kinds of" sales professionals, accountants, lawyers, doctors, executives, and retired persons. But when I asked if there were more of one than the other, he wasn't sure. We investigated. Over one-third were accountants and CPAs. About one-third mortgage brokers, and the remaining one-third a mixed bag. Now I want you to think about what use we might make of that piece of information, and we'll return to it a bit later.

Scenario #3: I have a client, SellMoreImplants.com, that does detailed data analysis and data mining for dental practices. They start by looking at all the information on file about the dentist's past implant patients, plus they use data common to implant patients in his fee range known from other practices they've assisted, and additional sources. With all this, they build a multi-data-point profile of the most likely potential implant patient for the dentist. Now I want you to think about what use we might make of that piece of information, and we'll return to it a bit later.

How to Use Information

Go back to the first example, the foreign brides business. With the information uncovered, here's what he could do: First, radically alter the places he advertised, and the amounts of money allocated to different places. There are magazines for and read only by truck drivers, truck stops where literature can be distributed, mailing lists. So, instead of spending 100 percent of the ad dollars in general media like *USA TODAY*, at least half could go where half the clients are coming from. In the Kennedy Marketing Triangle, I've just addressed Market and Media. Today, there are also Facebook groups and a plethora of other social media. Email lists. Second, he could take all his generic ads, sales letters, testimonial booklets, etc., and tweak them, creating a version talking only to and about truck drivers, featuring only testimonials from truck drivers. In the Triangle, that's Message. This gets to a perfect, tight Message to Market to Media MATCH. It strips considerable waste from ad spend.

Consider the second example—obvious now, isn't it? There are magazines for and read only by accountants and CPAs, mailing lists, associations, meetings, and conferences. The trade journals also have their own online media. There are email lists. Same kind of Media change, same kind of Message change.

Now, the third example. First, the data scientists at SellMoreImplants.com can go into all the dentist's past and present patient files and identify and—pardon pun—extract those that match most or all of the profile. Second, they can match the profile with online media like Facebook. Third, they can go to the commercial mailing list market to rent lists that match the profile. Then, fourth, they can go from a general, generic Message about implants talking to anybody who might need them to a precision-targeted Message talking to the individual profiled.

All three scenarios teach the same lessons. The WHO is very, very important. If you know WHO you want to attract, you can often find media or lists that reach only them. Often, the right description of WHO already exists in your business and you just haven't paid any attention to it or thought about how to use it.

Now, let's talk about outcomes. In Scenario #1, great price elasticity was discovered coupled with a LOWER cost per client acquired because of the efficiency of Message–Market–Media Match. Income roughly tripled year over year. In Scenario #2, price was doubled inside the niches of accountants and CPAs, sales costs lowered, and importantly, there were fewer telephone conversations leading to the sale, which means fewer tele-reps needed, and, overall, better quality, more capable buyers obtained. In Scenario #3, the typical dental practice using SellMoreImplants.com's program doubles or triples its number of implant patients in 12 months.

This is the power of information, *leveraged.* With untargeted advertising, you are buying giant, useless haystacks in which there are only a few gold needles to be found that are a good potential match to your business, for whom you can present a hyper-relevant message. With very targeted advertising and marketing, using the leverage of information, you buy a smaller stack entirely comprised of gold needles.

But what if you're new in business and have no backlog of data about your WHO? Try common sense. Maybe check your trade association or even competitors for some clues to WHO. Or, at least, start out with your own preferences. WHO do you want as client or customer? One way or another, get out of the anybody 'n everybody place at your earliest opportunity.

Personally, I long ago discovered that my best clients, best coaching group members, and highest value customers were politically conservative males from everywhere but the East Coast "blue states." Are there exceptions? Yes, and in sizable numbers—I have, and have had, great women clients, a few flaming liberal clients, and very good clients from New York. But the majority are conservative males, mostly from the Midwest, South, and Southwest. Consequently, I make no attempt to be all-inclusive in what I write, say, or produce, nor do I give even a minute's thought to who I might offend in the lower value, lower percentage groups. I know my prime Market and I design my Messages and choose my Media accordingly. The very best customers' or members' entry point is books, like this one, which is why I've written so many, keep writing them, and have considerable amounts of time and treasure invested in promoting them. The core of my business is the *No B.S. Marketing Letter*, a monthly newsletter, so, naturally, my best customer owns a business, is interested in marketing, reads, and will pay for information—all evidenced when he roams around a bookstore or goes to Amazon and buys one of my books. In short, I understand my ideal WHO, and I know the best media to reach him with. My understanding, specificity, and Message–Market–Media Match grew more and more sophisticated over the years. I started with: WHO was available and, of them, WHO did I want?

A point: It is perfectly okay for you to want certain people as your customer, client, or patient, and to NOT want certain people. It is your business. It is also your life, and it's too short to suffer earning your income having to deal with people you don't like or that you can't communicate with candidly or that don't appreciate and respect your expertise. There are all sorts of laws about "discrimination" that you dare not run afoul of, and this book is not legal advice. But with Message–Market– Media Match, you can *essentially* discriminate ahead of legal discrimination, by the Market you select, the Message you present, and the Media you use.

At bare minimum, let this chapter make you think more about Markets. Too many businesspeople think about themselves, their products, their services, and what they want to say about all that, rather than thinking about WHO is likely to be hungriest, most eager, most receptive, readily and affordably reachable, that they'll enjoy doing business with.

Let me VERY clear: As long as you refuse to dig in and become sophisticated and smart about selection and target marketing so as to clone and attract ideal customers, clients, or patients, there are three bad things that will remain true for you: 1) you will be conforming to what the majority of average businesspeople do, therefore 2) you will be prohibited from rising above the average income the majority of businesspeople earn, therefore 3) you will be unprotected from and perennially vulnerable to commoditization, competition, and income disruption by recession or other adverse circumstances.

Resource Alert!

The book *The Direct-Mail Solution* by Craig Simpson, to which I contributed, takes you down the rabbit hole to the Wonderland of lists, the commercial list marketplace, and deeply into all aspects of successful direct-mail. Craig is my "go-to guy" for lists and direct-mail project management, as he is for many of my top clients and groups of clients. He is often instrumental in doubling or tripling positive results. You can access Craig's information at Simpson-Direct.com.

What I have described to you here in this introduction to list selection and target marketing is not simple, but it's not impossibly complicated either; it's not easy, but it's not impossibly hard either. If a guy in the business of finding foreign brides, if a marketer of a business opportunity, if the owner of a local brick-and-mortar service business like a dental practice can figure out how to identify and then directly aim at and attract their ideal customers, so can you.

Message
How to Speak Magnetically to Your Chosen Market

You put out Marketing Messages constantly—whether you're fully conscious about it or not. People ask you "What do you do?" and you answer them. You spend money advertising your business. You communicate with current customers. It's important to understand five things about all this communication:

1. Your customers and prospects are buried in communication from your competitors and from countless others competing for their attention, if not their money. They are connected 24/7/365, but connection is not the same as engagement. In fact, consumers are, by necessity, practicing *active disengagement*. It is all a very dense fog to penetrate. Ordinary messaging won't do it.

   I wrote the above paragraph in 2013. Ten years later, it is 10X truer!

2. Most communication intended to interest customers fails miserably. Most net response from online or offline marketing is in fractions of a single percentage point. Marketers using my methods don't just do incrementally better, but often 200 percent, 500 percent, 1,000 percent

better. That is never accomplished easily or casually, nor by normal methods, and it shouldn't be. The effort to learn and switch to Direct Marketing is worth it.

3. Communication about products and services, about what you want to sell, is generally a lot more interesting to you than to your customers and would-be customers.

4. People are most interested in what interests them.

5. People are most easily and quickly interested in *information* directly related to what interests them— especially information that promises fascinating secrets, solutions to problems, prevention for dire threats, promises of seductive benefits or timely "breaking news."

Item 5 is the breakthrough prescription for magnetic communication.

Getting "Information-First Marketing" Right

I coined the term "Information-First Marketing" to *completely* separate what I do from what everybody else does, and to *completely* separate the advertising, marketing, and promotion of information first for magnetic attraction from all other, ordinary advertising of businesses and companies, brands, products, and services.

A good way to think about information you may create and offer is as bait. And a key principle is: MATCH BAIT TO CRITTER. If you want a yard full of deer, do not put a 50-pound block of cheddar cheese outside. Put a big salt block. If you want rats and mice, try the cheese. If you want to catch trout, do not tie an old shoe to your fishing line. Very simple formula.

Once you pick the critter you want to attract, as we just discussed (i.e., Market), you can then pick or create the right bait. In marketing, "bait" means two things: your Message and whatever "thing" you offer to spark direct response, whether that's literature and information, a free service, or a gift of one kind or another.

Most businesspeople get poor results from their advertising and marketing because they either put out no bait, lousy bait, or the wrong bait for the critters they hope to attract.

No bait, that's ordinary image or brand advertising, rather than Direct-Response Advertising. Lousy bait is boring, uninteresting, unappealing bait. A free report on *How to Buy Insurance* is lousy bait. A free report on *How to Outfox the IRS and Legally Avoid All Estate Taxes* might be better bait—for the right critter. That free report combined with a free audio CD with an interview with five wealthy executives, about tax planning mistakes they were making and how they fixed them, and another free report, *How to Double Tax-Free Yield on IRAs & Other Retirement Funds*, makes for better bait. Wrong bait for wrong critters—the free report on estate taxes, if you want to attract young married couples. Or if you are wasting money advertising anyplace where young married couples read, watch, listen, or congregate.

Media
How to Deliver a Magnetic Message to Your Chosen Audience

The list of media choices is longer than all the pages of this book ripped apart and laid end to end. The online choices keep expanding at a rabbit-breeding pace. Some appear mighty but then quickly die or are murdered by younger replacements—like MySpace and Yahoo. Remember when they were all the rage? I don't think there is any inevitability here. There is huge hazard for time and money suck, should you decide you must be everywhere, use all of it, keep up with its demands, regardless of measured results. It's funny to me, by the way, that nobody ever makes that decision about all offline media, but many succumb to it with online media.

There are newspapers, magazines, free-standing inserts, TV, radio, coupons, postcards, flyers, sales letters, catalogs, billboards, vehicle signs, bus bench signs, sky-writing, package inserts, imprinted golf tees, websites, email, social media—Facebook, LinkedIn, etc., blogs, YouTube videos, faxes, telemarketing and website addresses tattooed on boxers' heads or strippers' body parts, and thousands of variations and other choices. What's good? What's bad? What's best? What's worst? Is any of it essential?

No simple answer. Sorry.

First, it varies a lot by business. But more importantly, it has to do with WHO you are trying to reach. Do they pay attention to and respond to the media? A flyer for two-for-one pizza stuffed under windshield wipers of cars at a swap meet may be a good media. A flyer about investing at least $250,000 in international currency funds stuffed under the same windshield wipers, bad media. But it's not the media. It's the use of it. The one sure thing is this: If the media can't be used to deliver a *direct-response* message, skip it. If the media is not favored by your target market, skip it.

Warning: The media you or your staff prefer using, the ways you and they communicate and access information and entertainment, and your and their ideas about what *nobody* does anymore or what *everybody* does now does not mean squat. Only what your target customer audience actually prefers and engages with and obtains information they value from matters.

With that said, your mandate is to try to find ways to use as many different media as you possibly can. Most business owners become lazily dependent on only one, two, three means of getting customers, leaving themselves vulnerable to sudden business disruption and entry of more aggressive competition. With media, diversity equals stability. The more varied media you have working for you, the more protected you are from disruption, the more stable and secure your inflow of customers is.

CHAPTER 11

The **SECRET** to Infinitely Higher Response

The Dale Carnegie Secret on Steroids

by Dan Kennedy

Y ou have probably, at some point in your life, read Dale Carnegie's classic book *How to Win Friends and Influence People*. If not, you should. You may even be a graduate of the Dale Carnegie Program, as hundreds of thousands, maybe millions of people, are. It is, by far, the most enduring and successful course on communication, influence, attraction, and persuasion, period. At its core, the simplest of truths: One, people are more interested in themselves than in anyone or anything else; two, people want to be valued, respected, treated as important, and catered to; three, each person believes himself, his business, his situation, his needs to be *unique*—and is most responsive to someone who acknowledges that and is somehow well-matched or expert in that *unique* scenario.

When you move this to Direct Marketing, you can inject it with steroids and make it unbelievably powerful. And, as you'll see in this chapter's examples, you can gain incredible competitive advantage, because few business owners are willing to customize their presentations for different audiences.

Here, first, on page 125, I have reprinted four samples of relatively simple direct-response postcards used in the property/casualty/commercial insurance business by Gordon Quinton. You're not seeing both sides, you're not seeing everything, but you are seeing enough. Here are some of his reported return on investment statistics, using only the first year, direct value of the clients obtained (not including subsequent years' value or referrals):

Septic Contractors	$13 income for $1 spent / 1,300 percent ROI
Optometrists	$3 to $1 / 300 percent ROI
Apt. Bldg. Owners	$7 to $1 / 700 percent ROI

I imagine business insurance is, pretty much, business insurance, but Gordon has made himself and what he offers precision matched to each type of prospective client. The optometrists get an entirely different postcard than do the HVAC contractors than do apartment building owners, etc. Gordon customizes the headline, the "compare rates" examples, photos, testimonials, even his own business's domain name for each niche. And there is further congruent customization, as he has a separate and different website for each niche, too. Hopefully, you instantly grasp how very different this is from most business insurance brokers' and agents' marketing—typically, one big, broad, sloppy, and therefore uninteresting and ordinary message for all. Even brokers and agents in his area who see all this won't copycat it, because it's too much trouble. But then, nobody in his entire industry is ever going

Figure 11.1: Gordon Quinton, from the *No B.S. Marketing Letter*, October 2012

to see 300 percent to 1,300 percent returns on marketing dollars either.

One more example, from a chiropractor, Dr. Ken Vinton. Dr. Ken practices in a town of just 8,200 people. The month he provided me with the full-page newspaper ad shown to you here, in pieces by necessity, on pages 127 and 128, he topped his best month in many years of practice, in large part thanks to this ad. What's important is that Ken is not running a traditional, broad 'n sloppy, everything-chiropractic-done-here, for anybody 'n everybody ad. Not at all. Instead, he is targeting, calling out to, and speaking to *sufferers of chronic and severe pain who have tried medical treatment and OTC products unsuccessfully AND are being urged to go under the surgeon's knife.* He has crafted a specific Message for a very specific prospective patient, with full knowledge that others will be quickly disinterested in this ad.

So, you have a B2B and a consumer marketing example, demonstrating that the very same principles, strategies, and tactics apply in either sphere. Both of these examples, in their own way, demonstrate "the Dale Carnegie Secret on Steroids." There is no reason you can't figure out and capitalize on this secret as well.

On a related note, I've done a monstrous amount of research, and gathered great actual examples, for books about two very specific demographic/psychographic target markets: one, boomers and seniors; the other, affluent consumers. Like a business niche that Gordon chooses to Message-Market Match to, or a group of severe back pain sufferers flirting with last resort surgery that Dr. Vinton addresses, these groups have their own tribal language, their own key interests, their own turn-ons and turn-offs.

The affluent and ultra-affluent market could be very important to you as a safer, higher ground in coming economic storms. My book *No B.S. Marketing to the Affluent* gives you complete guidance in appealing to and attracting more valuable customers, clients, or patients.

The boomer and senior market IS going to be important to you. Starting in 2018, more than 50 percent of adult consumers in the U.S. will be over age 60, and they'll control 70 percent of discretionary spending. The Age/Profit Wave will determine

Figure 11.2: Example, Dr. Ken Vinton, From the *No B.S. Marketing Letter*

Example, Dr. Ken Vinton, From the *No B.S. Marketing Letter* Continued…

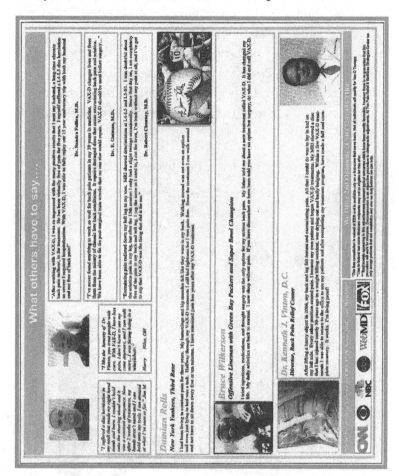

the fate of almost every business, directly or indirectly. My book *No B.S. Guide to Marketing to Leading-Edge Boomers and Seniors* is your guide to winning with this consumer population.

Available at All Fine Booksellers.

Notes: These Examples—as well as all other Examples in this book—are copyright protected by their owners, used here with permission, but otherwise all rights reserved. Copying them in whole or large part or their copy verbatim is in violation of U.S. copyright law and can subject you to civil and criminal penalties. The examples in this chapter first appeared in the *No B.S. Marketing Letter.*

CHAPTER 12

What's NEW?

by Dan Kennedy

J im Rohn said if someone invites you to visit their factory where they make new antiques, watch your wallet! Same with new fundamentals.

Nothing "new" has changed the fundamental Principles of Direct Marketing. You can read an antique book on this, like Claude Hopkins' *Scientific Advertising* (1923) and see for yourself. We have many, many more tools than existed in Claude's time to do scientific advertising, but the principles are unchanged.

Principles govern Strategies, and Strategies rule Tactics, and Tactics prescribe appropriate Tools and Technology.

But, you say, *something* MUST be new.

There is:

- New and more technology
- New advertising and marketing media
- New distribution channels
- New consumers and consumer preferences
- New, expanded, deeper availability of data

All this can provide new and improved opportunities OR new distractions and delusions.

I was advised that people could be disappointed if I revised this book without personally commenting on these things, so here goes:

New and More Technology

My business life divides about 50/50, pre-internet and post-internet. It is inarguable that all the media, all the marketing automation, the destruction of privacy and increased availability of data provided by the internet has been and is very powerful. In many ways, it has removed expensive barriers to entry, lowered ad spend costs, and facilitated new forms of word-of-mouth marketing. It has, however, also produced new kinds of gatekeepers—like portal sites, like Angi—and unleashed a woefully chaotic competitive environment via easy search, erased barriers to entry, and an inability for consumers to judge but by price. It giveth AND it taketh away.

But is it REALLY new? No. eBay is a drive-in theater's parking lot swap meet. Google is the Yellow Pages. Email is "junk mail." And so on. We are not doing new marketing functions or activities with it or because of it. We are doing the same things differently.

New Advertising and Marketing Media

I am a media agnostic. I am "for" anything and everything that works, productively and profitably, for your business. I'm usually "for" anything and everything that brings new customers, patients, clients, or donors at your MAC (Maximum Allowable Cost)—NOT just the least front-end costly of many. I have reasons to favor offline media vs. online, notably including the opportunity for evergreen campaigns and the avoidance of "search," competition, and commoditization. But I am not "against" online media. I doubt that coating myself in strawberry jam and twerking, naked, on a beach ball will bring me ANY good customers even if it brings me millions of viewers, but if you can prove that it does bring you valuable customers—twerk away!

The one strong caution I have is: Do not abandon "old" or legacy media just because it is old. That's dumb. As I write this (2023), I can show you local businesses getting outstanding return on investment from Yellow Pages Directory advertising and even national marketers using these directories every place they still exist. Just because you don't even get or have one, and ask Alexa for everything, does not mean there aren't a lot of good customers for you who don't. AM radio has become a favorite media for national direct-response advertisers and should be used by local businesses in the same ways. TV is still a great accelerant to fame and fortune. Being the author of a book showcasing your expert authority and promoting it successfully is still important. A book book. Printed, bound.

New Distribution Channels

I witnessed the birth and infancy of HSN, the Home Shopping Network, and behind it QVC. For many inventors, manufacturers, purveyors of all sorts of products, including some of my clients, this distribution channel was the opportunity that made them rich. Although new to TV, it wasn't *really* new. It was/is the old Sears mail-order catalog or the Macy's Department Store that had sex with Home Party Selling.

Amazon offers both devilish competition, but also a new distribution channel: Amazon Stores. And Amazon is, importantly, "Google *for buyers*." Having an Amazon Store has proven to be productive and profitable for many merchants, including clients of mine. Local businesses have gone global by this means. This has its drawbacks and isn't right for everybody, but it is new. But it's not *really* new. Amazon is the everything store. Nothing more or less.

New Consumers and Consumer Preferences

There are new consumers with each generation and demographic group. While each one tends to exhibit different preferences for how they buy and how they are sold to, it's dangerous to make easy assumptions. As an example, both Millennials and Gen X are exceptionally responsive to relevant direct-mail, contrary to popular assumption and opinion. It's important to get facts, not opinions or assumptions.

What does not change is basic human nature—why people buy. How people choose who to trust. The fundamental psychology of advertising is unchanged.

New, Expanded Availability of Data

The most recent generations have been willing, even eager, to trade away every last piece of privacy for convenience. As a result, there is more consumer data—demographic, psychographic, behavioral, purchase related—than ever before in my lifetime. There is even live-time data from some social media—the wedding planner can be alerted of women showing off their new engagement rings on certain social media as they do it. Data matching, to find customers that mirror current customers, is now available to small businesses just as it has previously been to big businesses. The co-author of the *NO B.S. GUIDE TO MARKETING AUTOMATION*, Parthiv Shah, is a premier data scientist. He offers a number of free resources at eLaunchers.com.

None of this is *totally* new. Commercially available mailing lists referenced at SRDS.com have long been a rich trove of consumer data and a tool for consumer matching, based on the disappearance of privacy. Still is. Lots of public information has always been available in compiled lists available for rent—like homeowners with home values of "x," incomes of "x," married, with kids, by occupation of head of household.

If It's New to You, It's New

Columbus didn't discover a new land. It had been there for quite some time. It was even already inhabited.

Your opportunities to switch to Direct Marketing and reinvent or revolutionize your business by doing so may be new to you. That doesn't mean the opportunities are new. To the contrary, they're all well-proven. We hope, through this book, you will discover opportunities new to you!

* Releasing in the Fall of 2024

SECTION 2

APPLICATIONS
& EXAMPLES

CHAPTER 13

Five Application
Breakthroughs

by Darcy Juarez

My journey of discovery of Direct Marketing for ALL Businesses is a lot different than most of you reading this book. I didn't own my own business and I wasn't struggling to find new customers. In 2003, I started working with a coaching business and that was how I was introduced to Dan Kennedy and Direct-Response Marketing. Like a lot of people reading this book, I didn't have any formal marketing training. In a way that made it a lot easier for me. I didn't have to unlearn any bad habits. The only thing I knew *was* Direct-Response Marketing. I read all of the books, I went to the events, I religiously read the *No B.S. Marketing Letter* (which is included in the free gift at the end of the book). I witnessed firsthand the power of Direct-Response Marketing and I was hooked. In 2011, I was offered the Director of Marketing position at Glazer-Kennedy Insider's

Circle, which is now Magnetic Marketing. This is where I saw how many businesses were changed by the principles in this book. I have worked with my own clients, been employed by different companies, and coached/trained at all levels. I have worked with brick-and-mortar businesses, product-based businesses, service-based businesses, and coaching and consulting businesses. The most successful all have one thing in common—they switched and converted to Direct-Response Marketing. Today, at Magnetic Marketing, I share all this with tens of thousands of business owners and entrepreneurs every year and directly work, hands-on, with hundreds. This doesn't just change their incomes; it changes their lives.

In the following pages, I'm sharing FIVE APPLICATION BREAKTHROUGHS that I have learned that have had the biggest impact on me and the businesses that I work with. While you may or may not be in the same business or same line of business, I promise that everyone can use these Breakthroughs.

Breakthrough #1:
Remove All Assumptions and Create
Clarity in Your Marketing Messaging

If the only thing that you did was focus on these two things, you could easily double any business. Too often, marketing messages are confusing and make too many assumptions. If you are not clear on why a prospect should choose to work with you, if you are not clear on what problem you solve, if you are not clear on how you solve that problem, how can you expect a prospective customer, client, or patient to be confident in choosing you? CONFUSED MINDS DON'T BUY. If there is too much confusion or too much friction, prospective customers won't choose you. It's very difficult to create a strong marketing and sales message when you don't have clarity. So the first thing needed is clarity.

What you do, why you do it, how you do it differently than anybody else, what chief and secondary benefits do you provide, why should I choose you versus other choices, why should I trust you about this...? All questions that must be answered, not ignored. Answered succinctly, forcefully, and clearly. Then, on top of that, what should I do, how should I do it, and why should I do it immediately, to engage with you? That's what makes the message a direct-response message: clear instructions for response.

The second big mistake is assuming *anything*.

1: Assuming that because you are good at what you do, new customers will flock to you. Maybe that thinking worked when there were only two options to choose from. Today the number of options in any category or niche is overwhelming. Everyone claims to be good, as good, better. Being good is just the ante to get into the game. It's just the starting point. We must do everything we can to persuade our ideal customer that not only are we good—but that we are *the only choice for them.*

2: Assuming that because you offered something for free, customers will say yes. I remember hearing Dan say that you often have to SELL free harder than you do other offers—you can't just assume that because it's free people will automatically say yes. An offer that seems too good to be true raises skepticism and doubt. In one business I worked with, they had a "free consultation" as their main offer. They thought that by just saying you can sign up for a free consultation that prospects should be flocking to say yes. But that is not how humans behave. The red flags go up and they associate a free consultation with a veiled sales call. So I renamed it from a "free consultation" to a "Free Double Your Production Strategy Session." I created a multi-page sales letter to sell the prospect on why they needed to drop everything and schedule this call. This included: what would happen on the call, why that was important to them, how others (like them) succeed in what was being promised (social proof), why now was the right time to be on the call, and what they needed to do to apply for their strategy session. I focused on reversing the risk because I knew they would come to this page or letter very skeptical. One of the subheads was "Are You Worried That Your Time Will Be Wasted?" and called out the elephant in the room by stating "we know that you are skeptical and thinking that the phone call will be nothing more than a sales pitch." And finally, a guarantee was included. Yes, I guaranteed a free call. **In Example #1 you can see the guarantee that was used. In Example #2 you can see the "what will happen on the call" copy selling the free consultation.**

(Examples on Pages 158.)

3: Assuming knowledge on customers' part. What is common knowledge to you is new and foreign to them. The person in need of an attorney for the first time is a stranger in a strange land and, compounding his disorientation, he may be having the worst week of his life. Same with most customers, clients, or patients with a new need or desire. Any assumption by you about what "everybody knows" can put up a roadblock and have them turn away.

4: Assuming that customers will remember to do business with you. It's not your customers' job to remember to do business with you—it's your job to remind them. So many business owners focus on the new customer and forget about the one they just worked so hard to acquire. An existing customer is the easiest customer to sell to. They already know, like, and trust you. When I go into a business, I am always looking for what is the next thing we can sell to existing customers. For every problem that we solve, we create a new problem. If a client is coming to me because they need more new customers and I solve that problem, it will create a new problem—now they don't have time to service all the new customers AND do the marketing to continue to attract new customers. So now, I can create a new product or service to solve this new problem. It might be how to hire a team to take over the delivery so that the owner can focus on growing the business. Then, once they have a new team hired (problem solved), there will be a new problem that emerges because they don't know how to lead the team (new opportunity). The mistake I see most often is thinking that everything needs to be included in the first offer to a new client. In one coaching business, when I first came in, every time we came up with something new to offer, their first reaction was to include it for their members. Instead, I started charging for the new products and services that were created each time a new opportunity arose. In doing this, we increased the one-year value of every new client by $4,000.

This is important for every type of business: What can you do or bring or offer to increase your average, yearly customer value? How can you communicate on an ongoing basis and episodically to increase your average, yearly customer value? The more valuable you make each existing customer, the fewer new customers you must get, and the more net profit you'll have.

Here's an example of getting this wrong. A chain of hardware and home goods stores has a good offer for the summer season: If you buy any of their backyard grills, free delivery and assembly is included, and you get a $50 gift certificate from the local upscale grocery chain's butcher shops. They mass-advertise this with expensive TV ads, newspaper inserts, and online, in social media. But they do not single out their regular customers who already look to them from time to time for products for the home but have never bought a grill from them, and deliver this offer—or a slightly better "VIP" version of it—direct to them, by an invitation mailed, even a postcard mailed, by an email campaign, or by telemarketing. This is a huge financial mistake. There is a fact of direct-response: A buyer is a buyer is a buyer. They have a list of buyers. But they are using all their ad dollars and marketing efforts aimed at a giant universe of non-buyers with a few potential buyers in it. Presenting a great offer to their buyers would be much more financially efficient.

Breakthrough #2:
It All Starts with the WHO, Not WHAT

I heard Dan say, communicate who you are and what you do so your WHO wants to and prefers to do business with you and only you. As I started putting together marketing messages and creating marketing assets, it really hit home how important the WHO is. When I tried to create winning marketing pieces without clarity on the WHO, they always failed. I realized that I had to go back and do the homework to create clarity around WHO we were trying to attract. When I consult with business owners, the first question I ask is, "Who is your WHO?" Who are you trying to attract? If that is not clear, the marketing message won't be clear. Your offer won't be irresistible, and you won't be able to emotionally connect to the ideal client. Words matter. The difference between a few different descriptions can radically change who is attracted. For example, one message was expressed as "if you are worried about making payroll . . ." Well, that attracted people who were worried about making payroll, and if they were worried about making payroll they didn't have a lot of money to invest in coaching, so the sale became a lot more difficult. When that was changed to, "if you are nervous about your cash flow..." the person we attracted changed. This person had cash flow; they were forward thinking enough to see trends and realize that those trends were making them nervous. They were more entrepreneurial and strategically focused and a better fit to invest in coaching. I didn't change what was offered or the price; I created clarity around WHO was being attracted. Demographic information about WHO we wanted to attract was easy—the harder pieces were the emotional and psychographic ones. But these were the pieces that spoke directly to the person I wanted to attract. And when that person heard the message, they felt an immediate connection. When we started attracting the right WHO, the sale became easier and the clients were more fun to work with. **Example #3 is a visual piece that I create for each business, so that everyone on the team knows who our WHO is (page 159).**

Breakthrough #3:
Ascension Is the Best Form of Retention

When you run a membership or coaching business, retention is usually a sore subject and one that has everyone looking for an easy button. The magic email, the magic onboarding script, the magic membership deliverable that stops members from quitting. In coaching, we don't have a physical pain of disconnect like the utility companies do. No one wants to quit the electric company. But for us, a member could wake up any day and decide that they were done, and many did before or when their initial commitment was up. In one membership coaching business I worked with, we took the retention from 10 percent to 72 percent. It wasn't done through a magic pill, or magic script, but instead a framework that started with the premise I heard Dan say over and over again: "Ascension is the best form of retention."

This can be and has been replicated in different kinds of businesses and has produced the same great results. We had people coming to us to solve a problem. But unless and until we showed them a bigger picture, and a bigger future, beyond that initial problem, they would leave when they believed they had solved that initial problem. Nothing we could say or do seemed to fix that. We have been programmed from childhood for ascension. Each year we graduated to the next grade in school. In swimming lessons we progressed through different levels. In martial arts we worked toward the next belt. No one wants to stay in first grade for three to five years, or in the same martial arts class for 10 years. And they didn't want that from our coaching program either. And they don't want that from your business either.

Someone buying hearing aids has a hearing problem they want to solve, and that is going to be the *obvious* focus of that sale. The less obvious, bigger-picture motivations may be "better hearing health for life" and "stay independent and capable for life." Unfortunately, there's no real opportunity to tie that to a ladder of ascension and a path of progression in that business, but in many businesses there is. Disney ascends people who stay in their hotels at Disney World to owners of time-shares at those resorts—i.e., Disney Vacation Club Members. They further ascend them by selling them bundles of extra points or a second home property, so the person with one time-share based at Animal Kingdom Lodge might buy a second one at the Polynesian Resort, doubling the time spent there each year. There's even an ultimate ascension: luxury home ownership at Disney's Golden Oaks. If your restaurant sold Gold, Diamond, and Platinum Memberships, do you think you could use that to increase frequency of visits, decrease that customer's random patronage of other restaurants, and improve overall customer retention? I can promise you, yes.

What we did was broken down into three areas:

1. Attraction of the *Right* **Person**

Dan had hammered home that success would be greatly determined by attracting the right people, not just anybody, and that they would need to have both the ability and the willingness to buy. The retention of the client started with how and what we attracted a new client with. Our lead magnets (see callout below) and their titles were critically important to attract the right person. We wanted to start with the right people raising their hand, not just anybody. This is why having an informative, curiosity-arousing book as a lead magnet was so important for us. We were dealing with a highly analytical ideal client. They needed a lot of information to feel like they were making a good decision. Our lead magnets weren't just any information; they were strategically created to connect where the prospective client was today to the bigger future that they wanted.

A LEAD MAGNET is an item, most often an information item or items, such as a book, special report, audio or video CD / DVD / online access, or package of several of these items as an "Information Kit"–those of us in the Kennedy World refer to these as Shock 'n Awe Packages. If you will watch direct-response TV ads, you will see Lead Magnets used commonly. As of this writing, several of the biggest direct-response advertisers on TV include Rosland Capital (gold) with actor William Devane, AAG (reverse mortgages) with Tom Selleck, and Fisher Investments. Fisher, for example, offers three Reports, together as a "Retirement Income Kit."

When we delivered the book, I wanted to make sure that it cut through the clutter. It was mailed in a bright shiny envelope—it wasn't an e-book or digital download. The perception of a real book arriving was important; it was a piece of the positioning that was done intentionally. A real book, one that is available on Amazon and/or bookstores, starts to lay the foundation and create ACE (authority, credibility, and expertise). I want the recipient to come to the conclusion that this is the right person to lead them through their problem to the solution that they seek. The biggest expense in mailing is the cost of the postage, so why not include as much as possible? I add more credibility and trust building marketing assets to the mailing. I included a piece that I call "Secrets of Their Success," which are testimonials on steroids. It's case studies of people like them who have achieved the results that they seek, but not just the testimonials—they are interwoven with the secrets that allowed them to achieve their success. Those secrets are what are taught in the paid program. There is a gift certificate to the next step in the process. I want them to have a physical piece where there is more space to really sell the importance of that step—I don't want to leave anything up to chance. I had another report entitled "Why Are We Working Harder and Not Making Any More Money?" which was one of their chief complaints. In it, I included a section on who we are and why that's important to the prospect. There was another section to overcome many of their biggest objections and points of skepticism. And then I justified the claims made in marketing with stories of success and I showcased other authority markers like a podcast and other books written. The last piece was a visual representation of how they would get from where they are to where they want to go. This allows them to find themselves in the process (**Example #4 is one of the maps; Page 159**). These are important pieces that alone may not have a big impact, but when combined with the next two parts are critically important.

Resource Alert!

If you would like to see Examples of these kinds of lead magnets and marketing assets, you can see a brief show-n-tell video at DirectMarketingFreeToolKit.com.

2. Conversion As a Process—Not a Sales Call

When a lead scheduled an appointment for a conversation (the next step), they were immediately sent via FedEx the shock-and-awe package. This is a concept I learned from Dan and he spells it out in his book *No B.S. Trust-Based Marketing. The goal of this package was to prepare the prospect for the meeting so that they arrived at a 7 or 8 out of 10 on a readiness-to-buy spectrum.* Included was a handwritten note. Because no one takes the time to handwrite anything anymore, this was a powerful piece. It was one of the most talked-about pieces, with comments like, "Thank you!" and "How thoughtful of you." We knew that we were not the only company that they were talking to so everything we did to show up differently and be different was important. Another key piece that was included was another marketing asset— the levels of membership. This one-page document showed the journey that members go on and how that related to their problems, frustrations, and where they were stuck. This one piece had the biggest impact on retention and ascension. It was a conversation starter—clients asking about each of the levels and how they could participate. It changes everything when people ask you how they can move up or pay more for a different level of membership versus you having to sell them on the same.

We did a split-test. There was a marked difference between those prospects who received a shock-and-awe package and those who didn't. Those who did, arrived at the conversation with a different demeanor. They were less skeptical, more open-minded, more respectful, and more appreciative of the time spent to customize and send them an abundance of information. They arrived already aware of who we were and felt like they knew us and believed that we cared about their success. They had come to their own decision about our credibility and expertise in the marketplace—we didn't have to sell them on this. There was a level of trust already established. This allowed for a quicker conversation and acceptance of the prescribed solution, thus shortening the sales cycle.

This approach replaces some tedious manual labor with media, reduces sales resistance and difficulty for the salesperson or business owner or practice professional, supports price or fee elasticity, and, as I said, can shorten the weeks or months or number of meetings needed to make the sale.

The sales call or sales conversation itself was designed and scripted to move them from thinking that this will be a one-and-done solution and instead opening their eyes to *a journey* they could embark on. We showcased the future and what happens past the initial problem they are coming for while still selling the solution that they wanted. We were planting seeds for ascension and a long-term partnership. Creating a shared, exciting vision of their future.

3. Delivery of Service

The minute a client joins, there is emotional angst and second-guessing that they may have made a bad decision. The way in which they made their decision to buy became very apparent during the delivery stage. A client who came in already prepared, meaning they were attracted through the above-described sales process, came in confident in their decision and ready to get to work. The clients who came in unprepared and hadn't received the above process were emotional and still questioning their decision. More time was spent reselling the deliverables that they had purchased. This group was more likely to quit. It was like the difference between a helicopter and an airplane ride. The unprepared client joins like the helicopter. They jump in and it raises straight up off the ground hovering at lower levels, never able to reach the higher altitudes. Whereas the prepared client joins more like an airplane ride. You board slowly, the plane uses a runway to prepare for takeoff, and ascends up at an angle, thus allowing it to reach higher altitudes. The way that a client is attracted and sold has a huge impact on their retention and ascension.

Delivery of the service that they bought isn't just about what they bought. The quicker we can start, the better. A "Welcome to the Family" box was sent out via overnight FedEx to arrive no later than two days after they joined. Like the shock-and-awe, they felt appreciated and that the delivery of the program was matching the investment they were making. Included was a leather binder with tabs. Inside the binder was their getting started information, but the blank tabs were important because they started a subconscious loop that there is more to come and their brains want to fill them in. Since most people never make a coaching decision in a vacuum, there are always employees, family, or friends impacted by the decision. We always included additional copies of our books so that those additional people felt included and understood why we did what we did. The key component was a questionnaire that was required for their first coaching call. Unlike most questionnaires that ask for business data, these questions allowed the new client to express their emotions, hopes, and dreams. **Example #5 showcases a few of those questions. (See page 160.)**

The questionnaire encouraged the new client to sit down and think about what they really wanted out of the program, why they joined, and what success will look like to them. Keep in mind, this applies to most businesses, not just the one I'm using as an example. When a customer, client, or patient "joins" your business, it's important for them and for you that they think through why they joined, what they want to get immediately and over time, and what success will look like to them. One of the best ad campaigns I've seen in the home improvement industry, for replacement windows, asserts that you will "LOVE your new windows so much you'll be eager to show them off to family, friends, and neighbors." Immediately after installation, the customer gets a "Celebration Box" with "I LOVE OUR NEW WINDOWS" t-shirts in different sizes, a bottle of champagne, gourmet chocolates, and a letter encouraging them to post photos and comments on social media.

Responses from our clients about the questionnaire were often, "This was so therapeutic," and "It really made me think about things I don't normally take the time to think about." What it did for us was expose their emotional hot buttons, worries, and fears and allowed us to tailor their coaching to have the biggest impact. People come for the logical tactics and solutions, but they stay for the emotional connection. This created fertile soil for future growth because things can't take root if you don't address the soil first. Sometimes it was more about the employees or personal relationships than it was about tactical implementation of key ideas. When those emotional pieces were addressed first, it was the equivalent of tilling the soil so that when they did implement the tactical-practical ideas, they felt more successful.

We also created a scorecard that allowed us to move a client from feeling to facts faster. Humans are naturally emotional beings and have emotional reactions to what is happening around them. And emotional responses often cause emotional reactions, like quitting. When the clients started receiving this scorecard prior to their coaching call, it changed the call from emotions and drama to focused conversations around facts and figures. The client felt more in control and focused on what will move them toward their future goal as opposed to reactive to what was happening in the moment. This produced a calmer and better client. They no longer felt like the sky was falling every day and it gave them confidence in the coach and the company. They could stay focused on the bigger future. They were less likely to quit because they were making strides toward their goal. They could see the progress made each month in black and white. The scorecard confirmed what they were promised in the marketing and during the sales conversation, thus building confidence in us, themselves, and their decisions. And when they had confidence in us, themselves, and their decisions—the choice to purchase the next product or service or ascend to the next level became a no-brainer. There was very little price resistance and very little "selling" needed because it was the next natural step. They started asking when they should or could take that next step. This allowed us to sell higher levels of membership, one that was double the price, with little to no marketing or selling needed.

If your business delivers progress over time—as with health care, weight loss, classes and lessons, new skill development—you have to *control* how the person feels about that progress. If retention over time is important, then, by some means, customers need to be scored and recognized or awarded for their longevity and loyalty. One of our longtime Members in investment real estate, Darin Garman, gives out a fancy Challenge Coin and published recognition to clients reaching either the five-year or $500,000-invested mark.

It was the focus on all three strategies that took the retention from 10 percent to 72 percent. It also tripled the average length of time a client stayed, and it quadrupled their value. The key was ALL PLAYERS HAD TO BE ON THE SAME PAGE, using the same verbiage, sharing the bigger journey (the future). Every time, every touch, everyone. The mistake made too often is that marketing sells one message, sales converts with a different message, and those delivering the services are focused on their delivery and not how it all fits together. Everyone doesn't understand why each piece is a part of the bigger puzzle. To have great retention and ease of ascension, it starts with the very first touch and continues through until the end.

Breakthrough #4:
Create Marketing Assets, Not Episodic Events

One of my first jobs was working at Kohl's in the juniors department. It entailed removing the clothes that were left behind in the changing rooms, refolding clothes that had been strewn about the display tables, and ensuring that there was half an inch of space between hangers on the racks. It was excruciatingly painful to me because as soon as I folded one table of shirts and moved on to the next, someone had come through and unfolded the ones I just folded. It was a never-ending cycle of doing the same thing over and over and over again. It seemed more efficient to me to just wait until the end of the day and do it once. I guess this is why I only lasted two weeks in retail. So when I heard Dan say that you should create marketing *assets* that will work for you day in and day out so that you don't have to constantly reinvent the wheel, it was like music to my ears. Redoing the work I had just done, just for the sake of doing it, was the bane of my existence. Instead, I could create a marketing asset (a sales letter, lead magnet, book, campaign, offer, website, webinar, etc.) and use it over and over again.

I think that a book is one of the best marketing assets for a coach, consultant, or any service business or professional practice, and is one of the first assets I like to create because it serves so many purposes. It creates credibility. On the surface, just the fact that you wrote the book and therefore you must be credible holds a lot of weight. Done right, it is a long-form sales letter selling the prospect on why you are *the* choice, *the only* choice to solve the problem that he specifically has. I can build multiple campaigns around the book. In one business, over a five-year period, I was able to attribute over $6 million in revenue directly to one book we wrote to attract the right lead and sell services. Different campaigns during those years, but all promoting that same book.

Marketing Assets Stacked

The real magic happens when you have multiple assets and you stack them one on top of the other to increase the power of each. In another business, we used a 60-day trial offer as our entry point. When I first went into that business, they had a proven offer but didn't have any assets to sell the membership outside of the offer. So the first thing I did was to create three emails to drive to the offer. I tested those with the house list, and once they produced results they became an asset. I knew that not everyone is ready to say yes to a trial membership, so the next thing I tested was a $5 offer for a bundle of resources with the option to add on the trial membership. Once that produced results, I had created another asset. About that time, the company started driving massive amounts of traffic into product launches with the goal to sell a $2,000 product, which came with a trial membership. If you know anything about product launches, you know that only about 1–3 percent of the traffic will purchase the product. I became obsessed with the 97–99 percent who didn't purchase the product. After all the selling was done, I took Asset #1 (three emails driving to the 60-day trial membership) and everyone who didn't purchase started receiving those emails. Five percent took the offer. Then I sent everyone who still hadn't responded to Asset #2. Twelve percent took that offer. What those percentages meant was that we had doubled the number of people taking the membership through the back-end offers as we had through the front-end offer (the product launch). None of that would have been possible if I didn't have two other assets available to stack. This can be done with any set of assets. I can stack up lead magnet campaigns, move from a lead magnet campaign to a webinar campaign, or stack proven offer assets. It all starts with creating marketing assets that can be deployed when and where I need them.

Dan often rails against marketing *as a verb*. As a daily job. Made even more high pressure by reliance on social media and online search, which demands new "content" constantly. This, he says, can certainly produce income, but it fails at creating equity. Only marketing assets—marketing as a noun—that can be continuously or repeatedly used build equity. In my work with business owners of every kind, I emphasize this point: Let's not get caught up in being new content producers for social media like laborers in somebody else's diamond mines. Let's BUILD ASSETS that labor for us!

Breakthrough #5:
Only in the Absence of Anything Else,
People WILL Make a Decision Based on Price

If you allow there to be an empty vacuum of information and ideas, price prevails. Prospective customers and clients don't have a lot of information to go off of when choosing a solution for their problem. When they call, they don't know what questions to ask. They don't know how to make a good buying decision. The only thing they know how to ask is: How much does it cost? I remember the first remodeling job I needed to hire a contractor for was to remodel the bathroom. Everyone I called scheduled an appointment for the next day to come out to the house and do an estimate. When they showed up, they handed me a business card and then emailed me the estimate a few days after that. That meant that to compare and choose a contractor, I had a business card and a price. That's what they provided me with to make my buying decision! Well, why wouldn't I choose the lowest-priced option? I didn't know why some were priced higher and lower than others. I didn't know how to tell a good contractor from a bad contractor. I didn't know what should be included in the price and what shouldn't be. I didn't know what to look for in the estimates. I was left to hunt for testimonials or reviews—so I did what most do. I googled and went to Yelp. One of the first things I do with every business is to create the marketing assets and design the sales process so that the prospective customer understands what a good buying decision looks like, they don't have to go hunting to find testimonials, and they have plenty of questions to ask that don't revolve around price.

It is easy for consumers to assume that every product or provider in a category is basically the same—and left with that assumption, they buy by price, and you die by price. There is opportunity in every category to sell at premium prices and profits, by creative and comprehensive differentiation.

Figure 13.1: Risk Free Guarantee

Figure 13.2: Free Strategy Session

Which is why you should accept my invitation to schedule a Free Double Your Production Strategy Session.

In only 45 minutes by phone, one of my top Production Specialists will create a customized blueprint for you so that you will know exactly what you need to do to double your production. No more guessing, no more wondering, no more wandering aimlessly. Here is what will happen on the call:

1. Using the data you provide; the production specialist will map out where your practice is now and the steps to get to where you want to go so you have a clear destination. It's like your own GPS system with step-by-step directions just for you.

2. They will uncover the 3 biggest areas of opportunity for your practice. These are never the same for every doctor, which is what can cause the most overwhelm and frustration. There is no cookie cutter map that every practice can follow.

3. They will suggest 2-3 new strategies, available to you immediately, that you are likely overlooking.

Once you have your roadmap, you can then decide to work with us or take the map and implement it yourself. Either way, you will leave the call with *your* roadmap to a practice that's enjoyable and profitable for *you*!

Figure 13.3: Appropriateness List

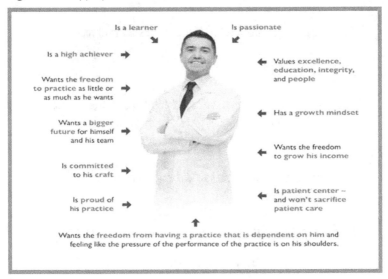

Figure 13.4: Four Stages

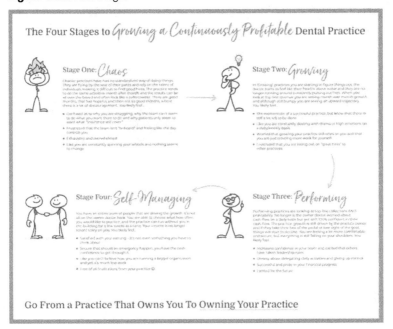

Figure 13.5: Questionnaire

What's going well in your business? What do customers like about your business?

What are your frustrations?

Have you worked with a consultant or coach before? If so, did you benefit from their advice? Is there anything they did (or failed to do) that annoyed or disappointed you?

A year from now, in order to look back and feel really good about what you have accomplished, what would need to occur?

Is there anything you can anticipate being a barrier or a threat to your success?

Is there anything you wouldn't feel comfortable with when it comes to growing your business/team/serving your customers?

CHAPTER 14

The Four Keys to My Direct Marketing Machine

by Marty Fort

From everything in this book, your task is to assemble your own Direct Marketing Machine for your business. "Machine" is important. It means that everything is operated in a machine-like way, not randomly.

The Machines that I have working for me today, for both my businesses, are quite sophisticated. I started doing this, though, on a very basic, even primitive, level.

My entry point to Direct Marketing was actually in my teens. It just came kind of naturally. I'm talking about when I was 16 years old playing in rock bands. I would book shows, create mailing list opt-ins (hard copy), and go out and solicit from the audience names, phone numbers, and snail mail addresses. There was no email at the time. There was no internet. I would take that information and put it into a spreadsheet. Then I'd make postcards and hand-address them to promote future shows and band news. I'd also do outbound calls inviting people on the list to the shows. In our mailings I'd give band offers: you know (showing my age but), free CD or cassette from the band, free T-shirt, free something. So, even when I was driving around in my Nissan Sentra (I've since upgraded) in my teens trying to build a following for the band, I always understood clearly so much of what you're learning from this book. That time in my life was my true entry point into Direct Marketing.

This was not unusual for big bands. They had fan clubs, newsletters, promotional mailings, swag catalogs. But for local "garage bands," this was very unusual. They just wanted to show up somewhere, get a paycheck for the gig, and play. This is still the major cause of failure for a lot of small businesspeople. They just want to hang up a sign above the shop door, show up, do their thing, and get paid for it by customers. They didn't open their restaurant or flower shop or dog grooming salon or architect office or dental practice to be in the marketing business. I correct this in the minds of as many as I can, with the music school owners I coach in the Music Success Academy and the work I do at Magnetic Marketing.

Fast-forward to my 20s, when I became a guitar teacher. I started the guitar teaching business with just myself and 30 students. I scaled it to a seven-figure multi-location music lesson *empire*! I've got 1,600 students in three locations and own commercial real estate / buildings for each. You can tour them online at ColumbiaArtsAcademy.com. So how did I do it? By using Direct Marketing for what is ordinarily NOT a direct marketing business. What were the primary items that created all of this success? I'd say the big ones for me were:

- Lists, Full Contact Information, Data Tracking
- Strong sales copy and specific offers with deadlines
- Great photos

There is no doubt that if you want to improve your Direct Marketing, top-notch, engaging photos help a lot. Especially in this day and age of online marketing. Also:

- Follow up
- Systems, systems, systems

Business Owner or Entrepreneur?

Consistent systems get consistent results and consistent income. They also liberate time, so you can be entrepreneurial. It is the autopilot marketing systems that liberated my time and allowed me to grow my first business from one to three schools and to expand with a second, synergistic business built from the first.

What's been really cool about studying and working with Dan is that he helped me transition into coaching and consulting. I formed an information business company over 15 years ago called Music Academy Success® (**www .MusicAcademySuccess.com**). It's the world's largest coaching program for music schools and music teachers. My company helps them with their human resources, management issues, real estate ownership, software, and an A–Z system of online, print, video, and audio trainings to help create a "Million Dollar Music School."

We Walk the Walk—Not Just Talk the Talk

With my three schools, we are all about Direct Marketing, so everything we teach and provide to school owners, we use successfully. Also, in attracting school owners, we use Direct Marketing, so they've experienced what we teach first by getting to know us.

One of the primary ways we obtain coaching clients is through Free Information Offers. The primary vehicle is our free report, which is called *The 16 Keys That Will Unlock the Hidden Profits in Your Music School.* This is a *60-page* (!) report done in print and online. You're sure to say: "Sixty pages? Are you kidding?" While the general attention span is short, the "interest span" of somebody who is a right fit for my—or your—proposition, and is intrigued and motivated to investigate it, is long. Joining my program is a significant decision, but then so is remodeling a kitchen or buying your first RV or taking your first cruise or picking your son or daughter's college. One of the key, contrarian strategies you'll learn as you become immersed in Direct Marketing is the use of *long* sales copy. Music Academy Success® is a high-end coaching program, and it is not "cheap." We offer true coaching, with direct access to me, live events, monthly group calls, a robust membership site, and more. School owners need to understand ALL of this to make the right decision. When you ask Dan how long a sales letter, free report, or other media piece should be, he always answers: "Long enough to make the best possible sales presentation, leaving no stone unturned."

You'll see on the next page examples from the Music Academy Success® *16 Keys* Report. You can see the entire Report at MusicAcademySuccess.com/report.

Of the 16 Keys, there are four of them that are absolutely universal, useful to any business:

Key #1, Understand That You Can Grow Your School to 300, 400, 500, 1,000 Students and Beyond

Presenting this Key, I'm trying to open up the school owners' minds to the possibilities of what can happen when we scale their businesses and switch to Direct Marketing.

There is probably some aspect of what you sell and the value that you deliver that needs people's minds opened, their

Figure 14.1: Music Academy Success® *16 Keys* Report

Dear Friend and Music Academy Owner:

Are You Frustrated By The Lack of Profit You Are Taking Home And Are You Ready To Do Something About It?

Hi, I'm Marty Fort and I've worked with music academy owners all over the world. From 44 U.S. states, including New York, New Jersey, Minnesota, California, Arizona, Washington, Colorado, Ohio, North Carolina, Wisconsin, Michigan, Oregon, Texas, Florida, Georgia, Illinois, Indiana, Virginia, Washington, DC, Oklahoma, Pennsylvania, Louisiana, Alabama, Tennessee, Nevada, to Canada, Europe, all over the world, to help them create a consistent and predictable system of enrolling all the students they need in their schools. Academies in major cities, such as Los Angeles and Dallas, use this system. Mid-size towns, like Tucson and Orlando, do so successfully. Smaller towns, such as Loveland, Colorado and Rogers, Minnesota, also use it. This system works in any area, regardless of the size of your market. Just like many of you, I have university degrees in music. I received a master's degree in classical guitar, toured Europe as a chamber music performer, lived in Los Angeles as an aspiring songwriter, even toured the southeast United States in a Judas Priest tribute band! I have been in the music teaching and performance industry for over 25 years.

(Pictured above left are my wife, Valerie, and our two dogs, Lucky and Mozzy. My school gives over $18,000 per year to our local animal shelter and has given over $100,000 total, since we started donating to them years ago.)

I even became a music professor for six years at the University of South Carolina Upstate until my music academy took off. Basically, like you, I had an extensive performing background, and then something happened . . . I hit the age of 30. It was time to start making some money and become successful in a business that would give me the lifestyle I wanted.

When I started my music academy I naively thought, since the instruction was good, that word of mouth would make me a success. I'd need a few flyers around town, a website, maybe a small ad in the phone book. I mean, how hard could it be?

After two years with no more than 50 students, I quickly learned **HOW HARD IT IS TO BECOME SUCCESSFUL IN THE MUSIC ACADEMY BUSINESS!**

Something had to change! I was getting married, and I needed money—now!

Figure 14.1 Continued

<u>Something had to change!</u> I was getting married, and I needed money—now!

I was making every advertising mistake in the book:
- I lost $2,000 to a local newspaper
- I lost $1,400 to another media source
- I had credit card debt
- I had a commercial lease hanging over my head
- My reputation was at stake!

<u>NOBODY THOUGHT I WOULD SUCCEED.</u>

The first step I took was this:

I Became A Serious Student of Marketing and Business.

I have received marketing awards in international competitions at some of the largest entrepreneur conferences. I was also featured recently on an audio CD talking about the success of my music academy and the marketing systems that I use. The CD went out to 25,000 small business owners worldwide. The great thing about Music Academy Success® is that we only talk about YOU, the music academy owner, and all the details unique to the industry that create success for music studio owners just like you.

- No dance studios.
- No gymnastics studio.
- No theatre groups.
- Music schools and teachers (many of them teaching in their homes) only.

Now, some of our clients offer those services and if you do, too, that's fine. Just please be aware that we don't discuss them in this program.

vision of what could be expanded. To consumers—parents— for our schools, we don't just provide music lessons; we build character, discipline, and study skills, and help create more confident, more successful young people. With our school owners, we get them to buy into this vision, making what they do more important and valuable.

In some of Dan's most advanced Training, he talks about the Power of PROFOUND Importance. Having Ajax as your plumber, checking everything on a regular schedule, preventing problems, but also on call 24/7/365 is not just about plumbing problems and solutions—it's about being able to take a second honeymoon or go on a great vacation or spend the holidays with your family and have complete peace of mind about your home being safe and secure. Not coming home to the horrendous flood your furniture is floating in. Revealing that your homeowner's insurance policy may not cover this at all or you may have a high deductible. The profound importance here is peace of mind. Doing the smart, responsible thing. And so on. Because Direct Marketing supports long sales messages and selling by story, these kinds of themes can be developed and used.

Key #2, You Have to Get a Better Grip on Your Money Math

Dan talks about money math in a lot of his books. His *NO B.S. RUTHLESS MANAGEMENT OF PEOPLE AND PROFITS* includes an in-depth discussion. To me, it's all about tracking. Tracking the meaningful, useful numbers, but also actually *understanding* the numbers, which ties into our Key #3 that I teach in the free report. We are showing school owners something new to most of them. This, too, is something you want to do with any business's marketing—show people something new, that they did not know, that your competitors aren't educating them about.

Key #3, They Have to Stop Losing So Many Students (Clients) Each Month (Loss Prevention IS Marketing)

When most school owners come to me as a new coaching client, I ask them how many students they're adding or losing. Too often their answer is…they have no clue. Or, they are letting the losses occur with no organized effort to stop them, while being over-focused on getting new customers. With the schools and with many other businesses, making retention a part of marketing and reducing losses can have a dramatic impact on profits. When I can get these owners to embrace Direct Marketing for retention, net profitability can double or even triple.

Key #4, You Can Make a Lot of Money during the Summer

One of the main principles that Dan's Renegade Millionaire System emphasizes is to do the opposite of what everybody else is doing in your industry. For example, in the music lesson industry, it's widely believed that you surrender during the summer break. Or just accept that you're going to go broke during the summer and starve until fall and back-to-school. But in my schools we have a system for making a lot of money in the summer. When we show this to other school owners, it's like showing fire to cavemen! I don't mean that disrespectfully. It is just so contrary to everything they've been told about their business, and then locked in as a "religious" belief about their business, that seeing it with proof that it works is mind-boggling.

This is something you want to achieve with your marketing, too: presenting something that is *mind-boggling*. Go ahead and contradict some existent, limiting belief your potential customers have, that your product or service blows up.

These are the four keys I use in both of my businesses. They can be integrated with Direct Marketing and used successfully in *any* business. Including yours.

CHAPTER 15

You Can Attract Your Ideal Customers, Clients, or Patients—Why Settle for Anything Else?

by Ben Glass

What can a lawyer teach you about marketing? What I learned about marketing literally changed my life and could change yours. No, unless you are a lawyer, you weren't looking for a chapter here filled with law practice marketing examples. After all, what do we pesky lawyers know about marketing except: run lots of ads with gory accident scenes and fistfuls of dollars? I don't blame you for your revulsion. I share it. As you'll soon see, I found a road less traveled. My experience may fundamentally change the way you think about what you sell.

We'll start, though, back where I began, with traditional, commonplace legal advertising.

Drug or product reported killing or maiming people? Throw millions at it in TV and print ads "warning" consumers about the dangers and side effects and advising that "you may be entitled to compensation!"

If your traditional lawyer marketing doesn't work, get "creative" and have cartoons showing yourself jumping over tall buildings or darting about in flying saucers.

Not dignified enough? Get "serious" and run ads showing the insurance companies "quaking" at the mere sound of your voice or mention of your name. Of course, you'd better be standing in front of those law books in your library when you create the ad!

Actually, if you are interested in marketing your professional practice, stick around and read this entire chapter. Here's why: There probably is not another professional services industry that spends, as a whole, as much on advertising as lawyers do. From websites to pay-per-click, from TV to radio, from print to billboards, lawyers hand over a ton of money to advertising reps, consultants, and to those selling the actual media. The competition among lawyers for new clients is enormous.

The legal profession is also the *second* most highly regulated professional services industry when it comes to advertising. (The financial advisors have it worse, but there is not nearly as much money being spent to capture a new financial client as there is for lawyers.)

In every town there's the 800-pound gorilla that's outspending everyone else, too. You see his picture on every park bench, bus, and billboard. If there's a Yellow Pages directory still published in your town, his face, together with an American flag, likely adorns the back cover.

So, if you are a lawyer, this chapter will help. If you are not a lawyer, this chapter will help even more because if I can help thousands of solo and small-firm lawyers compete against the 800-pound gorilla in their markets, and do so in an ethical, dignified way that helps many consumers get their problems solved, imagine what you can do in your industry where there is not nearly the level of money and sophistication being deployed by your competition.

If Lawyers Can Solve These Marketing Problems, Then It's Gonna Be a Piece of Cake for You in Your Business

Here's the problems lawyers face when it comes to getting new clients:

1. There's a ton of us out there and many are willing and able to spend massive amounts of money on marketing.
2. There was no marketing class in law school so we tend to just copy what other lawyers do, but do more of it.
3. Marketing is still, by and large, looked down upon by the established bar, and that segment of the bar tends to be the ones getting appointed to the committees that write the rules about advertising.
4. Most of what the public thinks they know about lawyers is derived from two sources: (a) the silly "monkey see, monkey do" lawyer ads they do see and (b) massive anti-lawyer campaigns financed by insurance companies and big business. If someone has had an experience with an attorney, there is about a 50-50 chance that it was a negative experience because the "event" was the resolution of a dispute and the adversarial process is just no fun. This means that we have a huge "trust barrier" to overcome as well.

Here's the Old Way Lawyers Solved the Problem of Breaking Through the Clutter

Here's the ad I ran when I first opened my own practice.

Figure 15.1: Example Law Office Ad

Look familiar? Of course it does. It's the same ad that nearly everyone runs in any business. It's the ad that says, "I sure hope that by some random chance this ad provokes you to call me." Of course, I copied the ad from someone else, but the yellow page rep selling me the ad said it was a "good one." She was the expert. What the heck did I know?

I was very proud of this ad and ran it for several years after I had left my old firm, where I had worked for 12 years to start my own law practice in 1995.

Think it was a winner? Let me put it this way: The only people who called me from that ad were: 1) loser potential clients who had already been told "no" by all the other lawyers in the phone book, and 2) marketing vultures who saw me as an easy sell for their ads.

I struggled, because while I had developed a successful track record as a young attorney and had won several important (and big) cases, there still was no good way for a potential client who might be looking for me to find me. Even if they found me, there was no good way for me to differentiate myself in this very crowded and competitive marketplace. I couldn't think of a better way to say "Free Consultation" and "We Care."

Magnetic Marketing Changed My Life

One day in early 2003, I got a letter in the mail offering Dan Kennedy's "Magnetic Marketing" course. It was a long letter that promised that, no matter what my business, I could market myself so that I would have a long line of people begging me to represent them. The letter hit on all of the problem spots that I outlined above. It talked about being seen as a commodity and constantly lowering my standards to service every person who called looking for a lawyer. I bit on the sales letter, and ordered Dan's program.

This was my introduction to Direct Marketing.

When the big box containing a huge three-ring binder and audio tapes (this was pre-CDs) arrived, I dove right in. I freely admit that after going through the tapes and the binder several times, I still understood only about half of what Dan was talking about and I didn't even have a real good idea of exactly what "direct marketing" was, but I do distinctly remember thinking to myself that:

If I could figure out how to use what Dan and his Magnetic Marketing Course was talking about in my law practice, it would change everything.

I did figure it out.

Today, not only has my law practice (BenGlassLaw.com) boomed but I've created a huge information marketing business

(GreatLegalMarketing.com) that teaches lawyers in all different practice areas and in every part of the country how to more effectively market and build their practices. No more talking frogs and flying saucers for us!

Let me take you through the steps that we now use to market BenGlassLaw (BenGlassLaw.com). Our small firm now has 13 branch offices throughout much of Virginia. All of the growth is driven by Direct-Response Marketing. It's the only marketing we do. Clients come to me "pre-sold." They often speak of already "knowing me" from reading my books, watching my DVDs, and viewing many online videos.

Your job, when you get through this chapter and the rest of this book, is to figure out how you can use what's here to market your business. You need to be smart enough to translate "client" to "patient" or "customer."

Five Secrets to Using Direct-Response Marketing to Market Your Professional Practice

1. Identify your "perfect client" before you do anything.
2. No matter how much or how little the prospect knows about you or your services, create irresistible offers that literally compel them to say: "Market to me more."
3. Don't buy more ads—instead, get "in front of" your competition.
4. Embrace the complexity of marketing and work hard to develop marketing that talks to your best prospects no matter where they are on the "moving parade of interest."
5. Develop a follow-up system because the real treasure is buried there.

Secret #1: Identify Your "Perfect Client" before You Start to Market

If you have clients right now in your office who are making your life miserable, you have only yourself to blame! Your marketing attracted them and your fear that you'd never get another client let them in the door when they came a-knocking!

You must start by clearly identifying who you want to see walking through that door. My friend Matt Zagula, co-author with Dan of *No B.S. Trust-Based Marketing*, calls his perfect client in the financial services industry his "avatar client." Both Matt and I have "drawn" the image of our favorite type of client in our minds, put that image on paper, and have created marketing that is specifically designed to attract only that type of client.

Remember, I'm a personal injury lawyer. You might say, "Ben, how could there be a 'profile' of a 'perfect' personal injury client?" After all, car hits car, it's pretty random, isn't it? Don't personal injury lawyers want to represent everybody?

Lawyers who don't know anything about marketing do say they want to represent "everybody," but that's only because they don't know any better. They are also the first ones to complain about all the undesirable clients whose files bark at them from the file cabinet.

My perfect client is someone who is middle to upper class, educated, has plenty of car and health insurance, and is looking for a respected authority (and not just a lottery payout) from whom they will take advice. Of course, we are also looking for large damages cases, and we are not shy about saying that. My marketing is designed to attract that client and to repel anyone who doesn't match that model.

For a little bit of "inside baseball," here's a list of attributes that I don't want to see in a client:

- Thinks their injury is the path to riches.
- Claims that it's the "principle that matters" and they aren't really "interested in the money."
- Is on their third lawyer for this case and first wants to talk about "how their other two lawyers screwed up a great case."
- Wants to instruct me on the law and the value of their case.
- Wants to make sure the defendant pays with their own blood (in addition to any insurance money).
- Has had multiple accidents and a history of pain in the same area where pain is claimed now.
- Claims a large injury but bumper on car shows only a scratch.
- Wants to collect for lost wages but hasn't paid taxes in years.

My "perfect" may not be your "perfect," but you need to know who your "perfect" is or you'll be back to attracting everyone with your "free consultation" or lowest price type marketing.

Secret #2: Create Offers That Compel Them to Be Interested in More Marketing Messages from You

No matter how much or how little the prospect knows about you or your services, you must never again develop any marketing piece that doesn't invite your prospect to contact you to request even more information from you.

The very best marketers in any industry do not have just one information offer for each product/service. They have multiple offers, each masterfully created with this thought in mind: The potential client may know nothing about what I am selling; they may know "A" but not "B"; they may have already researched the product/service a lot; or they may be seeing you at the beginning of their research.

As we will see, prospective clients go through a multi-step decision-making process. You never know, because *they* (not you) control when and where they enter your world, what they've seen, heard about, or believe before they notice you for the first time. Were you having this discussion with them "live" in their living room or your office, this would be easy. You could gauge where they are in the buying process and adjust your presentation accordingly.

The key is to offer something of real value to them right up front. We do it with a number of free books they can download and videos they can watch. This starts to build trust but also tells them that there is "more behind the door" and all they have to do is ask for it.

Secret #3: *It's a Fool's Game to Try to Simply Outspend Your Competition — You Need to Get in Front of the Crowd of Competitors by Shouting a Different Message*

Most lawyers wait until someone has already made the decision to hire an attorney before they begin to market to them. That's why most lawyer ads are all about the experience or "caring attitude" or reputation of the lawyer.

Thinking of nothing better than "**Dewey, Cheatum, and Howe, We Care for You and Offer Free Consultations**," most lawyers then try to beat the competition by simply buying more ads. This is risky, expensive, and dumb.

First, waiting until someone has decided to find a lawyer is too late. You can actually begin to market to potential clients (and get them to listen to you) before they have reached that point. We do it with this message:

If you have been injured in an accident, you may not need an attorney. But, before you 1) talk to the insurance adjuster, 2) hire an attorney, or 3) sign any forms, contact us, and get our free consumer guides.

With our free information you will learn 1) how to avoid the five major mistakes that new accident victims make with an insurance adjuster, and 2) how to find the right lawyer for your case.

You see, we know what is running through our prospect's mind just after an accident. For example, they want to know a couple of things shortly after they've been in an accident:

1. Should I talk to the insurance adjuster who keeps calling and give the recorded statement he keeps bugging me about?
2. Should I sign the insurance forms they keep sending over? What about accident-related forms my own insurance company wants me to sign?
3. Can I handle this on my own or do I need to hire an attorney right away?
4. Which insurance company will pay my mounting doctor bills?

Our initial messaging says to a consumer: Wait, slow down, don't panic. We can help you BEFORE you decide if you even need an attorney or not. That's what I mean by "getting in front of the crowd."

Secret #4: Embrace the Complexity of Good Marketing and Work Hard to Develop Marketing That Talks to Your Best Prospects No Matter Where They Are on the "Moving Parade of Interest"

The "moving parade of interest" is a term I first learned from Dan Kennedy. It means that your prospects go through a process when making a hiring decision. The problem for you is that you can't control where they are along that "moving parade" when they first notice you.

Think of it this way. The last time you bought a new car you likely didn't just wake up one day and say 1) I want a new car, *and* 2) it's going to be a Lexus, *and* 3) it's going to be silver, *and* 4) it's got to have a premium sound system.

Unless your old car was totaled in an accident, you went on a "decision path" that likely went something like this:

1. My old car is looking a bit dull.
2. I deserve a new car.
3. I can afford the new car I deserve.
4. I like the following brands: Lexus, BMW, Ford.
5. OK, I really like the Lexus.
6. Wow, there's all these Lexus ads on TV.
7. Let's visit the Lexus website where I can "design my own car."
8. Let's go for a test drive.
9. OK, I've decided I want the RX 350.
10. Let's see where in town I can get the best deal on the Silver RX 350 with premium sound.

If a car dealer is doing a good job with their marketing, they are going to develop messages and marketing materials

(DVDs, online videos, testimonials) that address you no matter where you are and push you to the next level until you convince yourself that the silver Lexus RX 350 must have been built with just you in mind!

This is where it gets complex. (*Mindset note:* Embrace the complexity. Your competition is lazy. Do this work.) You need to create marketing messages that speak to your prospects wherever they are. Here are some examples in my world:

- In an accident and have literally no clue as to what do next. (Free download of my book at www.TheAccidentBook .com.)
- Have some clue about what do to but want to try to settle the case themselves. (Free download at www .GetItSettled.com.)
- Have learned that trying to settle the claim themselves is more complicated than they thought and want to hire an attorney but don't have a clue as to how to choose one lawyer over another. (Free download at www .TheTruthAboutLawyerAds.com.)
- Like everything they see about us, but made the mistake of hiring another lawyer before they saw us and want to fire that lawyer. (Free download at www .FireMyAttorney.com.)
- Had a case before but didn't get as much money as they could have because they bought the wrong type or amount of car insurance. (Free download at www .TheInsuranceBook.com.)
- Have a very specific question about some small part of the whole claims process? (We've probably answered it at www.LegalAcademyVideos.com.)

Those are the steps for grabbing the interest of a person no matter where they are on the "moving parade of interest."

Remember, though, you *must* create marketing like this for each of your practice areas. The questions and concerns that a divorce client has are different from someone who was arrested last night and different from the guy who was in a car accident. One size does NOT fit all.

Yes, it took a lot of work to produce all that content and I haven't even shown you the follow-up that "backs up" each point of entry. Embrace it!

Secret #5: Develop a Follow-Up System because the Real Treasure Is Buried There

All we have really done so far is to get the attention of someone who may be a prospect for you. No matter where they were in their thinking when they discovered your message, you've now had them identify themselves to you and you have been given some level of permission to market to them.

This is huge! Congratulate yourself.

Now we reel them in with a comprehensive follow-up campaign that provides overwhelming proof that you are the wise man at the top of the mountain.

"Oh, Ben, more work! Are you crazy?"

Nope. Here's what we know not only from my own practice but from the feedback we get from thousands of lawyers who listen to me in every type of practice area and in every type of market: An extensive multi-step, multimedia marketing campaign directed to someone who is now paying attention to you is the Holy Grail of marketing.

Don't wimp out now!

No matter where along the "moving parade of interest" a prospect is when they first ask for information, they are going to get one of our free instant downloads and an invitation to get "more" for a trade of full contact information from them.

When they give us full contact information and enough evidence that they've actually been in a car accident in Virginia, then they are going to get our "Ben Glass Law Shock and Awe Package." We tell them to be on the lookout for it. This big envelope contains a number of our books, a TV interview on DVD, a radio interview on CD, and a number of other free reports that that will be helpful to them.

We follow this up with more mailed packages—books with more books and free reports. Of course, there is also a series of auto responder emails. The content of the emails differs depending on whether the prospect has told us that they are "just curious about what we are doing" (as you may indicate when you go to any of the URLs in this chapter and request information) or whether they have provided us with enough proof that they just might be a good prospect for us.

Warning: Do not make the mistake of relying on auto responder emails only! Nothing beats the mailman bringing a package to the prospect's house. Our marketing system is run with Infusionsoft. Frankly, we've found nothing better and have been a raving fan since 2005. (You can learn more at www.infusionsoft.com.)

Let me leave you with this fact from our own experience in switching all of our marketing in the law firm to Direct-Response Marketing (Kennedy-style):

> We discovered that our best clients hire us anywhere from 3 to 12 months *after* first entering one of our Direct-Response Marketing funnels. Our perfect client is taking the time to 1) heal from serious injuries and 2) do research before making the decision as to which lawyer to hire, and when they show up in our office

they are 3) usually carrying with them the big bundle of stuff we've sent them. Importantly, we are making more money and having more fun.

Now it's your turn. If my profession can do it, you've got no excuse.

Ben Glass is a practicing personal injury and medical malpractice attorney in Virginia. He is also the founder of Renegade Lawyer Marketing, and author of *How Today's Solo and Small Firm Lawyers Survive and Thrive in a World of Marketing Vultures, 800-Pound Gorillas,* and *Legal Zoom* (www .GreatLegalMarketingBook.com).

Ben can be found at: www.BenGlassLaw.com and www .GreatLegaMarketing.com.

CHAPTER 16

They All Laughed When I Stopped Selling My Product—Until I Became a Top Agent and Transformed My Entire Industry

by Craig Proctor

I f you're a serious student of direct-response headlines, you recognize the famous headline reworked as my chapter title. It's accurate, because just about every real estate agent and broker I knew when I literally stopped advertising and marketing myself and my properties *laughed*. When I started making the radical changes described in this chapter, I was all alone.

My story is about my real estate career, but I promise, there are eight breakthrough strategies here that can radically reinvent almost any business for the better.

I became the top RE/MAX® Agent in the world at age 29. For 22 years, I averaged selling a home every day! Along the way, other agents stopped laughing and started asking how I was achieving such extraordinary success. I've trained over

30,000 agents, and no less than Michael Gerber, best-selling author of the business book on system in business *The E-Myth,* characterized me as "a visionary who reinvented the job called real estate and teaches agents about freedom rather than about work." I'm the guy who brought Direct-Response Marketing to the real estate industry. I'm famous enough as a leader in the field that, in recent years, I've been copycatted and had my material taken and taught by quite a few people. I'm still innovating, though, so hundreds of agents who've been in my coaching programs for years continue and hundreds more join month by month.

This lofty perch seemed unimaginable when I began my real estate career. When I started out, I made the same fundamental mistake 99 percent of all beginners make—and many keep making forever. I looked around at how everybody else was doing it and simply copied them, striving to excel by outworking my competitors. This turned into a demoralizing period of my life. I spent my days and nights cold-calling, knocking on doors, doing floor time at the office, wasting weekends at open houses. I soon hated going to work to face repeated rejection. Most importantly, my real estate business wasn't working for me financially.

Eventually I got so sick and tired of nauseating and highly inefficient prospecting that I decided there had to be a better way, and, like many before me, I decided that this better way had to be advertising. Once I began advertising, I reasoned, my troubles would be over. Instead of me chasing prospects, prospects would now come flocking to me!

Well, that's not exactly what happened. Again, my strategy was to copy what those around me were doing. This led to very traditional ads—a big picture of me and a catchy slogan. You see ads like this every day in your own real estate publications, and you might ask yourself, "What's so wrong with these ads?"

The problem with self-image advertising is that the focus is on the "agent" when it really should be on the "customer."

My first ads may have drawn attention to me (see an awful example of my early advertising in Example 16.1), but they didn't get me business because they didn't offer prospects anything they cared about—there were no customer benefits or reasons for a prospect to contact me. Whether you know it or not, your prospects are all tuned to the same radio station:

Figure 16.1: A Great Example of a Really Bad Ad

WIFM (What's in it for me). If your ad can't answer this question, chances are your prospects won't bother to even look at your ad, let alone respond to it. Lesson learned. I found out the hard and expensive way that just because prospects know who you are doesn't mean they'll call you.

I needed to find a solution. The problem was, while prospecting bled me emotionally, image advertising bled me financially. I didn't know how to make this business work for me and I actually considered getting out of real estate, but since I had nowhere else to go, I was driven to figure it out. This was 1989 and I had just heard through a friend about a "marketing renegade" with a refreshing, but unorthodox approach to advertising. His name was Dan Kennedy, and I still remember seeing the picture of him sitting on a bull. How appropriate given this guy was positioned as "no B.S."

Dan introduced me to the concept of Direct-Response Advertising: the premise that every ad must be held accountable to garner an immediate and direct response; that every penny I spent on advertising must be trackable and therefore testable; that what was missing in in 99.9 percent of marketing campaigns was strategy.

As you'll see shortly, I aggressively applied this principle to all of my marketing, and the payoff for me was huge. What I realized is that not only were the ads that most agents placed not effective, but the strategic foundation of the entire industry was all wrong. There are really only two things that most real estate agents advertise: *themselves* and *houses*. I was no different, until I took a step back and analyzed what I really wanted my advertising to do to get prospects to call me. While that may sound self-evident, when I evaluated traditional industry ads against this mandate, I realized that they not only fell short; they actually did a much better job of *repelling* prospects than *attracting* them.

Breakthrough #1: The One Reason

My industry's mistakes with advertising are not at all unique. In fact, the majority of all advertising is about the advertiser or the product. My solutions also apply to many other kinds of businesses. The radical change I made—at the time, ahead of anyone else in my field—is one you can profit from as well.

The radical premise I committed to was and is: *The only reason* to advertise is to get prospects to call you.

Let's reject Image Advertising first. Even if you're not a real estate agent, you have most certainly seen these self-promotional ads where the agent paying for the ad talks about how great they are, their designations, how honest and hardworking they are, etc. Let me be clear about the fact that no one cares. Despite this, year in and year out, in every marketplace across the country, real estate agents waste vast sums of money on beautiful pictures of themselves with catchy slogans that no one pays attention to.

Breakthrough #2: Replace Image Ads with USP Ads

In stark contrast to ineffective Image Advertising, Dan introduced me to the concept of Unique Selling Proposition (USP), challenging me to answer for my real estate business the most important question on every prospect's mind—i.e., "Why should I do business with you versus all other options, including doing nothing at all?" This made total sense to me and I jumped all over it. I started to test different USP messages and quickly came up with a winner, which I aggressively used: "Your Home Sold in 120 Days or I'll Buy It." This very effectively positioned me as "the guy who'll buy your home if it doesn't sell," and this irresistible consumer benefit drove truckloads of business to my door like never before. I never looked back.

In a slowing Toronto real estate market in the early 1990s, my Guaranteed Home Sale Program helped me succeed because it solved a very important consumer problem. While every agent will promise to sell your home, I guaranteed it—a very meaningful and compelling consumer benefit (see Figure 16.2). In fact, several times a day the phone would ring with prospects asking: "How does this 'you'll buy my home thing' work?" To which I would reply: "I need to see your home before I can tell you how much I will buy it for." This of course made perfect sense to sellers and now I was face-to-face with someone who wanted to sell their home...always a good thing if you're a real estate agent.

Now I know what you're thinking—how the heck did I buy all of those homes? The truth is that during my entire 22-year real estate career I only bought two homes, and that occurred

Figure 16.2: A Rider on All My Signs Marketed My Powerful USP

when I broke my own rules. Over the past 20 years, I have been responsible for bringing the Guaranteed Sale Program mainstream by introducing the rules and conditions of this program to thousands of real estate agents in my seminars and coaching programs. You can get more information on the GSP and everything else I teach, including free training, at **www.NoBSRealEstateMarketing.com**. (*WARNING: Other seminar/training organizations have tried to copy what I created but don't really understand the inner workings of the GSP.*)

I have already discussed why Image Advertising is completely inefficient. By simply replacing my image ads with USP ads, I got an immediate and dramatic increase in sales. With USP advertising, I not only created massive awareness in my marketplace; I also successfully attached a very powerful and tangible consumer benefit to my identity, so not only did prospects know who I was; they also understood exactly what made me different and better than my competition, and they had a specific reason to call me.

This is the heart and soul of Direct-Response Advertising: a specific reason to respond to you.

The GSP is only one of the many successful strategies I teach real estate agents, but because it's *perceived* to be risky, this is NOT where I begin with agents who are new to *The Craig Proctor Real Estate Success System*.

I said there were two things that real estate agents traditionally advertise. The second is their property listings (products). In fact, millions of dollars are wasted every single day on this very ineffective strategy that most agents would agree nets them few results, certainly not enough to pay for the ads.

You may ask why agents keep doing this if it doesn't really work. Well, there are three reasons:

1. Every other agent does it this way so it seems like the right thing to do.
2. Agents don't have a better strategy to attract buyers.
3. Sellers demand it because other agents keep doing it, and on and on it goes.

None of those seemed like very good reasons to me, so I focused on discovering a better and more effective strategy. The solution I discovered to both better promote my listings and attract buyers changed my business virtually overnight. My secret formula is incredibly simple, and here it is:

Breakthrough #3: The Most Effective and Least Expensive Way to Generate Leads Is to Offer Prospects Something They Want and Make It Easy and Nonthreatening for Them to Get It

Ever since I understood the power of this simple principle, all my marketing has been built around it. In every single ad and marketing communication I invest in, I make the offer so appealing and so easy to get that the right prospects unfailingly respond by contacting me to do business. This is the essence of Direct-Response Marketing. It is marketing that causes your prospects to immediately act—to respond to you directly because they really want what you're offering. Remember, "the only reason to run an ad is to get prospects to contact you."

Pick up the classified section of your local paper, or browse Craigslist online under Homes for Sale to see what I mean. I want to make a very important point that I believe will shock many of you. The fact of the matter is, the role of a property ad, whether in print or online, is NOT to sell the house in the ad.

I'll go further than that and state: "It is virtually IMPOSSIBLE to sell a house with a classified ad." What happens MOST often is that a buyer calls about a listing, and as the agent begins to describe the property to them, the buyer begins to eliminate it and politely tells the agent that it's either too big or too small, in the wrong area, too much money or whatever and hangs up the phone. When I explain it in this way, agents can see that the ad doesn't often sell the house they are advertising. So, if it's next to impossible to sell the house in the ad, why do agents keep trying to do so by babbling on and on with lengthy descriptions of property features?

When agents are writing their classified ads, they shouldn't be thinking about how to showcase all the wonderful features of this house; instead, they should be thinking about how they can get the highest response.

So, what are the benefits that will be most motivating to prospects?

When you scan the classified section of almost any paper, you see that agents fill their ads with non-emotional property features: walk-in closets, new roof, central vacuum, etc., instead of using words that actually strike an emotional chord with buyers.

Let's take a look at two ad examples in Figure 16.3, which describe the exact same property. I think you'll agree that the property ad on the left is very typical of the kind of ads most agents run.

Staying for a moment with this typical agent ad, let's talk about the process of elimination. Agents inadvertently penalize themselves by adding eliminating words to their ads that actually cause prospects NOT to respond. For example, the ad on the left advertises that the house is a two-bedroom, and

Figure 16.3: Narrow vs. Wide Funnel

NARROW FUNNEL:
Example of a typical
"feature" driven ad (don't do this!)

NEWMARKET–2 bdrm, corner lot, closet organizers, garage door openers, water softener, new dishwasher, $279,900. Call (905) 830-1234. Bob Smith, XYZ Realty.

WIDE FUNNEL:
Example of a great "emotional-benefit"
direct response ad

NEWMARKET–Lovely Homes, quiet streets, great neighborhood. Free list with pics at www. NewmarketHomesList.com
Free recorded message 1-800-000-0000
ID:0000

there are many great prospects who will immediately eliminate this house as they feel it's too small. The same thing applies to a "corner lot." Some prospects like a corner lot but some don't. The ones who don't, will eliminate the ad. Elimination means they won't call the agent, which means the agent never gets a chance to tell them about different listings they would be interested in and thus, they never have a chance to convert the buyer to a client. So, as you can see, by focusing on the specific, unemotional features of a property, agents vastly limit the number of good prospects who will respond to their ad.

Breakthrough #4: Instead of Advertising What You "Have," Call Out to Your Prospects by Advertising What They "Want"

Let's look at the ad on the bottom of Figure 16.3 to help you understand the big innovation I brought to this industry. I've helped agents make more money by <u>NOT</u> advertising their listings.

My method stops agents from advertising "what they have"—i.e., their listings. What I've taught agents to do instead is to craft ads that call out to who they most want to attract. With this strategy, I teach agents to write ads that focus on who they want to attract instead of trying to sell the listing they have.

The fact is that agents are not enslaved to only sell their own listings. They can sell a buyer anything on MLS. So, instead of focusing their advertising on offering prospects only what they "have"—i.e., their listings—I've taught agents to offer what it is that prospects "want," and there's no rule that says the properties they offer have to be their own listings. More than anything else, what today's real estate consumers want is variety, choice, great deals, hard-to-find properties, AND they want accessing this information to be easy and nonthreatening. So I teach agents to give them exactly that. After all, it's very difficult to eliminate an entire list of homes.

Breakthrough #5: People Do NOT Want to Be Sold

Another very important thing I want you to notice about the ad on the bottom is that the call to action does NOT direct prospects to call "me." I teach agents to provide prospects a nonthreatening way to get the information they offer by driving prospects to a website and/or toll-free recorded hotline, both of which offer prospects the information they want in exchange for their contact info. I call these my automated robots because they automatically handle all prospect inquiries for me. The result? Now I have good quality leads to follow up with because the very nature of the information I offer (such as a list of homes) is only of interest to real prospects.

Most businesses have an opportunity to use this very same strategy—and it can change everything.

There are several important advantages to driving prospect inquiries to automated robots, such as a hotline or a website. From a marketing perspective, it has been proven that three times as many prospects will respond if they don't have to speak with a salesperson to get the information they're after. Why? Because people do NOT want to be sold. If you make a great offer but tell people they have to call a salesperson directly to get it, you'll significantly lower your response. Also, these robots give you the important ability to scientifically track every ad you run.

In addition to these marketing advantages, there's a huge lifestyle advantage to driving prospects to a website and/or hotline—one that will change your whole way of doing business. You see, with this strategy, the prospect is not actually calling the agent directly. Instead, they're calling to get the information offered in the ad, so prospects are not even expecting a call back from the agent. It *is* important that agents follow up with prospects so they can convert inquiries into a face-to-face appointment, but now—instead of the agent being interrupted with prospect inquiries 24/7—they simply call the prospect back when it's convenient for them.

Breakthrough #6: Replace Your Property (Product) Ads with My Wide-Funnel Ads That Offer Lists of Homes Your Prospects Cannot Eliminate

Imagine generating so much business that you can effectively raise the bar and ONLY work with the most sincere, most motivated, most ready-to-act prospects. Prospects that will work with you and not fight you. Using the simple, inexpensive little ads I developed, my students have been able to do exactly this. By using my ads to generate dozens of qualified leads week in and week out, they now have the luxury of choice and can pick and choose who they want to work with. They can set their own rules of engagement and do business on *their* terms.

Breakthrough #7: Increase Demand by Creating Competition and Urgency

Another innovation I'm known for is my reinvention of the traditional open house. The Old School approach has the agent open a home for three to four hours on Saturday and Sunday afternoons hoping and praying that a buyer will walk in the door and say, "WOW, this is the home of my dreams"—and then buy it. I'm not saying that this never happens, but it's a very low probability game (less than 1 percent of homes are ever sold in this way). In fact, if it happens, the agent just got rewarded for bad behavior and may be convinced to continue with this inefficient approach.

Early in my career, I wasted many weekends doing this exact thing. Sitting alone in a stranger's home does give one plenty of time to think, and what I sat and thought about was the same thing all entrepreneurs think about in times of crisis—i.e., "There must be a better way." So, on one of those Sunday afternoons all those years ago, as I sat at an open house, I was thinking about something my father had recently shared with me. My father has many rental properties and one night at dinner he shared his frustration of agreeing to meet with a prospective tenant, only to be stood up. Sick and tired of all the time he wasted on these no-shows, he finally said "no more" and changed his approach. Instead of meeting tenants individually, he decided to force all of the tenants to meet him at the rental property at the exact same time. Under this new scenario, he no longer cared if some of the prospects didn't show. As an added bonus, the many that did show were now competing for the one and only rental opportunity. My dad no longer had to sell the virtues of the rental property because tenants were literally throwing their deposits on the table.

I got to thinking that this same strategy just might work for me. So, the next weekend, instead of opening one home, I decided to open six of my listings on the same afternoon and the "Craig Proctor Sunday Tour of Homes" was born. I purposely forced all of the buyers to each home at the same time. Each home was open for exactly 10 minutes with 15 minutes of travel time between homes. So the first home was open from 1:00 to 1:10 p.m., the next home from 1:25 to 1:35, etc. I was able to conduct the entire event on my own because I could get from house to house in 15 minutes. Halfway through my very first Tour of Homes, I knew this was a game changer. Not only did many buyers show up at each home, but each buyer saw other buyers who also appeared interested and an "auction effect" was created. No more selling. My properties sold for more money in less time, buyers loved it, and for the next 18 years I never conducted a traditional open house again.

Breakthrough #8: Always Find Innovative Ways to Get Prospects Hunting You Rather Than You Chasing Them

Much of my success is the result of challenging and vastly improving on the traditional way things were done in my industry. This became a way of thinking for me and I want to share three more examples with you.

The Reverse Offer

This strategy helps agents get their sellers' home sold in a buyer's market. Traditionally, buyers view many listings before making an offer on a home. What that means, of course, is that only one seller is going to get the offer.

This is a very passive approach, and one in which the seller's odds of being the loser are much higher than their odds of winning. As a Plan B, what I teach agents to do is make a reverse offer, and here's how it works. When we list a property, we have the seller sign a purchase and sale agreement, complete with a good price, flexible terms, and a cover letter (which we call a Love Letter) from the seller. The Love Letter describes why the home is right for the buyers—the schools, the community, the church, and the neighbors—all positive. This offer is then packaged, and when a prospective buyer previews the home and is not forthcoming with an offer within 48 hours, my seller makes a reverse offer to the buyer. The offer gets sent over to the buyer's agent and presented as any offer would with a 48-hour expiration.

The worst-case scenario is that the buyer says no thanks, but often what happens is that the buyer says, "Well, I would buy the property at x..." The seller now knows the buyer's x and can respond accordingly—in essence, the buyer's counteroffer. You would be amazed at the number of buyers who are on the fence regarding one house or another. The problem is that they have the universe to choose from due to the high levels of homes for sale. A little nudge or "reverse offer" from the seller can often help them see through the overwhelming supply and develop a top-of-mind awareness of the seller's home.

Paying the Long-Distance Bill

As you can imagine, I sold a lot of real estate in my marketplace, a bedroom community called Newmarket, 30 minutes north of Toronto, Ontario. I wanted to find a way to give back to my community, while at the same time promoting myself. Traditionally, agents have done this by handing out notepads, pumpkin seeds, or calendars with their name on them. Most of this stuff ends up at the bottom of a drawer or in the garbage— another waste of an agent's money. I decided to do something different. At the time, a disadvantage of living in Newmarket was that residents had to dial long distance to call Toronto, something the average resident had to do a lot, at great expense (this was before all the cheap, North American–wide long-distance plans). So I promoted a special Toll-Free line (939-FREE) that enabled residents to call Toronto for free after listening to a 10-second message from me (I recorded several messages promoting my USPs, which rotated). This simple idea not only created massive goodwill and awareness; it also generated huge PR for me, both locally and nationally (I was featured in national newspapers and on national television news shows like *CBC Venture*).

Over-the-Phone Homeseller Seminar

Traditionally, agents conduct buyer and seller seminars at their offices or at a local hotel as a way of selling to many prospects at the same time. But remember Breakthrough #5—People Do NOT Want to Be Sold. What I did instead was offer an over-the-phone homeseller seminar as an easy and nonthreatening way to get my prospects to raise their hands. My ad for the over-the-phone seminar was designed to look like a public service announcement, and I asked a real estate lawyer and mortgage broker to join me to host the call. While callers were not asked to identify themselves in order to participate, each of the panelists offered a free report with valuable information that the most qualified seller prospects would crave. Of course, in order for prospects to receive these reports, they had to leave their contact information providing me a great lead to follow up with.

Real Estate done the traditional way is frequently difficult, unprofitable, and unrewarding for agents. No wonder 82 percent don't make it to their fifth anniversary and why there's such burn and churn in the industry. Agents who learn my system have an entirely different experience. They make much more money in far less time, giving them more freedom to do the things they really want to do.

If my innovative approach to this business intrigues you, there are many easy entry points to my system, which you'll see when you visit www.NoBSrealestateMarketing.com, but one of the simplest ways to get involved is to sign up for my FREE training programs and information that will allow you to test my system in your business and even benefit from live weekly training that will show you how to get started. If you can copy, you can succeed. My system has been responsible for the biggest success stories in the industry, with thousands of my members earning high six– and seven-figure incomes as a result of what they've learned from me. These are the top agents in the country. You could be next.

If you are not a real estate agent, I hope you'll think about my experiences and breakthroughs as a fill-in-the-blank challenge for your business. Push yourself to find an application of each of my eight breakthroughs. Just as I figured these out for myself to radically reinvent the real estate business, you can for your business, too.

Known within the industry as the King of Lead Generation, Craig Proctor (the top agent for RE/MAX® Worldwide for several years) not only sold over $1 billion of real estate himself in his 20+-year career, but he's also coached more agents to millionaire status than any other coach or trainer. While the cornerstone of Craig's system is lead generation using his famous "Reverse Prospecting," Craig's is a comprehensive system, which also includes highly effective scripts, conversion, and presentation systems to empower agents to follow their leads through to maximum profit. By openly sharing his step-by-step approach, Craig Proctor has trained over 30,000 agents worldwide on how to create a business that serves their lives providing them more money, more time, and more freedom.

Other Books in The NO B.S. Series

The Best of No B.S. (2022)

*No B.S. Guide to Direct Response Social Media Marketing
with Kim Walsh Phillips, Second Edition (2020)*

No B.S. Marketing to the Affluent, Third Edition (2019)

No B.S. Direct Marketing, Third Edition (2018)

No B.S. Time Management for Entrepreneurs, Third Edition (2017)

*No B.S. Guide to Powerful Presentations
with Dustin Mathews (2017)*

*No B.S. Guide to Maximum Referrals and Customer Retention
with Shaun Buck (2016)*

No B.S. Ruthless Management of People and Profits,
  Second Edition (2014)

No B.S. Guide to Brand-Building by Direct Response (2014)

No B.S. Trust Based Marketing with Matt Zagula (2012)

No B.S. Grassroots Marketing with Jeff Slutsky (2012)

No B.S. Guide to Marketing to Leading Edge Boomers & Seniors
  with Chip Kessler (2012)

No B.S. Price Strategy with Jason Marrs (2011)

No B.S. Business Success in the New Economy (2010)

No B.S. Sales Success in the New Economy (2010)

No B.S. Wealth Attraction in the New Economy (2010)

Forthcoming NO B.S. Books

No B.S. Time Management for Entrepreneurs, 4th Edition
  with Ben Glass

No B.S. Guide to Successful Marketing Automation
  with Parthiv Shah

No B.S. Guide to Growing a Business to Sell for Top Dollar
  with David Melrose

Other Books of Note by Dan S. Kennedy

Almost Alchemy: Make Any Business of Any Size Produce More with Fewer and Less (Forbes Books, 2019)

My Unfinished Business: Autobiographical Essays (Advantage, 2009)

The New Psycho-Cybernetics with Dr. Maxwell Maltz (Prentice-Hall Press, 2002)

AUDIO BOOKS are available at Audible.com.

Index

Want To Stand-Out Among Your Competitors?
Then You'll Want...

The Most Incredible FREE Gift Ever!!!

Learn How You Can Grab $19,997 Worth Of Pure Money-Making Information
FOR FREE!

Including a FREE "test-drive" of
Dan Kennedy's NO B.S. Letter!

Scan the QR code or go to:

DirectMarketingFreeGift.com

Printed in the USA
CPSIA information can be obtained
at www.ICGtesting.com
JSHW060357290524
63882JS00002B/1

9 781642 011685